Build Your Own PC

Fourth Edition

Build Your Own PC
Fourth Edition

Morris Rosenthal

McGraw-Hill/Osborne

New York   Chicago   San Francisco   Lisbon   London   Madrid   Mexico City
Milan   New Delhi   San Juan   Seoul   Singapore   Sydney   Toronto

The McGraw·Hill Companies

McGraw-Hill/Osborne
2100 Powell Street, 10th Floor
Emeryville, California 94608
U.S.A.

To arrange bulk purchase discounts for sales promotions, premiums, or fund-raisers, please contact **McGraw-Hill**/Osborne at the above address. For information on translations or book distributors outside the U.S.A., please see the International Contact Information page immediately following the index of this book.

Build Your Own PC, Fourth Edition

234567890 QPD QPD 0198765

ISBN 0-07-225559-5

Vice President & Group Publisher
Michael Hayes

Copy Editor
Marcia Baker

Vice President & Associate Publisher
Scott Grillo

Proofreader
Paul Tyler

Acquisitions Editor
Marjorie McAneny

Indexer
James Minkin

Project Editor
Patty Mon

Composition
Dick Schwartz, Jean Butterfield

Acquisitions Coordinator
Agatha Kim

Illustrators
Kathleen Edwards, Melinda Lytle

Technical Editor
Karen Weinstein

This book was composed with Corel VENTURA™ Publisher.

About the Author

Morris Rosenthal is a best-selling author and computer consultant. He holds degrees in electrical and computer engineering, has built or repaired thousands of PCs, and has trained numerous PC technicians. He's been featured on the Dateline NBC web site and in the national press as an expert on computer repair and technology purchasing issues. Rosenthal maintains one of the most popular independent computer-technology sites on the Internet at www.daileyint.com.

Contents at a Glance

Contents

Introduction

The purpose of this book is to get you building your own PC. The approach is to illustrate the process with hundreds of step-by-step photographs accompanied by specific assembly instructions. There are three complete build stories in this book, each illustrating a different family of technology. Some of the steps appear almost identical from system to system, but we vary the camera angles and the order in which the steps are done to cover as many bases as possible. The point is that we aren't going to leave out a crucial step or show you how to do something wrong, just for the sake of variety.

Chapter 1 contains a review of all the basic PC parts and their functions. Chapter 2 moves on to the subject of shopping for parts and understanding the dollars versus performance tradeoff. Chapter 3 presents information about handling and assembling PC parts, making standard connections, and some common pitfalls you can avoid. Chapter 4 is our first fully illustrated build, utilizing the latest Intel technology. Chapter 5 is a Athlon 64 system ideal for gamers and multimedia applications. In Chapter 6 we assemble a Pentium 4 system in a tower case with options for advanced storage solutions. Chapter 7 looks at a typical Windows XP installation. And, Chapter 8 consists of troubleshooting checklists in case you encounter problems getting your new PC running.

One of the hardest choices for the author of a PC book is whether or not to include pricing information, which changes faster than ink dries. While we include pricing for basic parts that will result in a complete PC with a price tag under $400 to high-performance parts that will add up to a system costing thousands of dollars, these amounts are entirely dependent on current market conditions. We do not offer competitive reviews or present "roundups" of competing components. This is the domain of PC magazines and web sites, some of which offer daily updates. This book does supply you with the vocabulary and examples needed to shop for ultra-high performance parts, but its primary focus is on the practical considerations of purchasing and assembling home PCs.

The toughest decision for a new PC builder is how much to spend on parts. If you're on a limited budget, be thankful, because once you know how much you're going to spend, the rest is easy. Until you make the dollars decision, shopping will be a nightmare. For every component you consider, there will be a faster one or a higher capacity unit available for just another $20 or $50. The next performance level can be reached for $75 or $100, and so on, until you reach the latest and greatest component in every category and exceed the limit on your credit card. Three months later you'll open the newspaper or be surfing the Web and see an ad for a PC with exactly the same capabilities as yours, but it will already be $500 less than the one you put together. Don't spend more now in hopes of keeping up with the future. Wait for the future and upgrade. Once you've built your own PC, you'll see how easily and cost-effectively you can upgrade if the need arises.

Chapter 1

First-Time Builders

This chapter is written for first-time PC builders who have limited experience with PC hardware. Our main focus here will be to supply you with the necessary tools to move on to the job of selecting and purchasing components. The main tool needed for this task is a genuine understanding of the vocabulary of PCs. Keep in mind that learning a new vocabulary is like learning a foreign language. You only need to memorize a couple of words to ask a question, but you need a degree of fluency to understand the answer. Feel free to skim or skip over any terms or parts you are already comfortable with. However, even if you've been using a PC longer than a microwave oven, you might find that you know less about what goes on inside than you thought. After all, how many people know that a microwave oven uses a 2.4 GHz (gigahertz) magnetron tube to heat the food, or why?

Speaking of gigahertz, now is as good a time as any to get the most basic part of PC vocabulary out of the way, the units of measure. Almost all PC components will have one or more units attached to them to describe storage capacity (bytes), speed (hertz, seconds), transfer rate (bits or bytes per second), power (watts), and visual properties (dots per inch, dot size). Most of these units are expressed in quantities of thousands, millions, and billions, or the reciprocal fractions (thousandths, millionths, and billionths).

The truth is you don't really need to remember the underlying foundation of these units to make informed decisions; it's only their relative weight that matters. Thus, a 200 GB (gigabyte) hard drive has four times as much storage capacity as a 50 GB hard drive. Both drives store many billions of bytes (1 GB = 1 billion bytes), but you don't need to worry about the value of a billion or the meaning of a byte to compare prices and pick a hard drive off the shelf. Just for the record, a byte can store a numerical value between 0 and 255, which can be interpreted as a letter or symbol according to a standard code.

The average word in this book is a little less than six bytes in length, and the smallest hard drive available can hold tens of thousands of full-length novels. The most important figure of merit for all computer parts is measured in the tens or hundreds—of dollars. Rather than presenting all the units associated with computer parts and expecting you to memorize them, we'll simply explain the units each time they are encountered and include them in a table at the end of the chapter for reference.

The basic parts in a computer are all dependent on each other to carry out their functions. For example, all the parts depend on the power supply for electrical current at the required voltage levels, and some parts, like the central processing unit and memory, are dependent on the motherboard (main circuit board) to further refine that power for them. This makes it difficult to explain the functions of these parts without referring to others, so we will tackle them in an order that minimizes confusion.

All in all, there are somewhere between ten and fifteen distinct parts involved in a PC build, including the monitor, keyboard, and mouse. By distinct parts, we mean components you pick off a store shelf or order over the phone or the Internet. Assembling all these parts to create a working PC will require you to make about ten push-together connections and screw in twenty or thirty screws, four here, six there, nothing complicated.

Case and Power Supply

The case is almost universally sold with the power supply installed and included in the price. You can build a PC on a workbench without a case (technicians often do this when testing parts), but it takes up a lot of space, interferes with the radio, and is awfully hard to pick up and move in one trip. The function of the case is to house all of the parts that make up your PC, provide ventilation for the heat they generate, and protect the local environment from radio frequency interference.

All electrical devices that produce radio frequency emissions are required by law to be certified by the Federal Communications Commission (FCC) as noninterfering with assigned broadcast frequencies. Computers produce a lot of radio frequency "noise" in the FM radio band and higher, but at very low power levels. Normally, if a computer in your home interferes with a radio or television, moving it to another room or even just changing its position by a couple of feet will fix the problem.

Computer parts are sold as being FCC Class A or B approved. Class A is for business use, the Class B rating meets more stringent limits for residential use. Assembling a collection of approved parts is no guarantee that the completed computer would pass an FCC test suite for one rating or the other, but as a home hobbyist, you aren't required to have your computer tested. However, if you decide you love building PCs so much that you want to go into business selling thousands of them, you'll probably want to buy partially assembled or packaged systems that come with an FCC approval sticker.

The power supply, which we lump together with the case because they are sold together, has two basic functions. The primary function is to supply electrical current to all the PC components at the proper, regulated voltage levels. Computer parts require a variety of direct current (DC) voltages, none of which exceed 12 volts, but the power supply itself operates on alternating current (VAC) from the wall socket, so you never want to remove the sealed cover or stick a screwdriver in through the fan grille.

Power supplies are equipped with a 115V/230V switch, so they can be set to 230 volts for Europe and most other regions of the world that don't use the U.S. standard 115 VAC distribution system. Just a few years ago, this 115 or 230 volts was wired directly to the switch on the front of the PC, like the switch on a lamp or a toaster oven. However, in all new PCs, the high voltage never leaves the power supply. The switch on the front panel is really just a logic switch that closes a circuit on the motherboard, which tells the power supply to come on at full power. The power supply is always providing a trickle of current to the motherboard to enable this "wake up" logic, whether the signal is generated by the power switch, or by incoming traffic to the modem or network card.

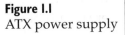
Figure 1.1
ATX power supply

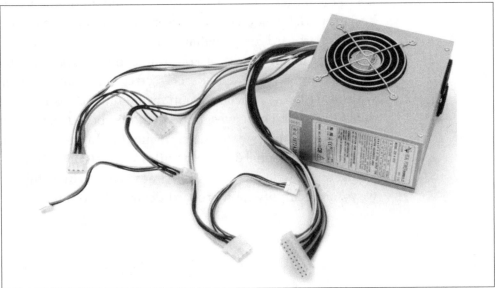

The second function of the power supply is to generate a cooling airflow for both itself and for the other parts in the case. This fan in the power supply is the main source of noise coming from most PCs. The manufacturers of the newest high-speed components often recommend that you include additional fans in the case to increase the cooling airflow. The most common location of a single additional fan is at the bottom of the front of the case, to draw in air. A second fan can be added under the power supply at the back of the PC to exhaust more hot air. The goal is always to increase the airflow through the case, not just to blow hot air in a circle, so don't install several fans to draw air into the case and none to exhaust it, or vice versa.

Motherboard

The motherboard, or *mainboard,* is normally the first component to be installed in the case. All additional adapters will be installed directly on the motherboard, and storage devices (drives) will be attached to it by special purpose cables. There are a dozen well-known motherboard manufacturers and hundreds of lesser-known brands. PCs are not named for their motherboards, but by their CPUs, such as Pentium 4 or Athlon 64. The CPU and the memory (RAM) require no connections to anything else in the case other than the motherboard, and can therefore be mounted on the motherboard before it is installed in the case. Not surprisingly, the motherboard is the largest component you will install in the case, and is often the most expensive.

The modern ATX (AT eXtension) motherboard provides many basic functions. It passes power from the power supply to the installed adapters, CPU, and memory modules; provides connection ports for the keyboard, mouse, and printer; and integrates all the supporting functions necessary to make the CPU into a computer. Most jobs handled by the motherboard go on entirely in the background, transparent to the user and remarked on only if there is a problem. The motherboard function that you should always keep in mind when building your PC is that it acts as the communications infrastructure for the entire computer. The motherboard is crisscrossed by information superhighways, some as wide as 64 lanes, which move information and instructions from one component to another. The newest trend in motherboard technology is to replace these multilane highways with the equivalent of high-speed rail, or bullet trains. A single, unidirectional data path with special signal conditioning can move individual bits of data more than 100 times faster than on the congested superhighways, and simplify motherboard design at the same time.

Figure I.2
Motherboard
I/O core

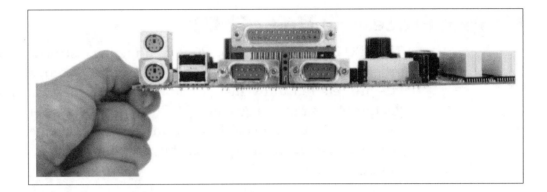

For example, to display a checkbook ledger stored on your system last week, the CPU (which does most of the decision making) asks the hard drive, via a motherboard superhighway, to send this information to immediate memory for use. The requested information is moved from the hard drive to the memory (RAM) via a motherboard superhighway, where the CPU operates on it via a special expressway and formats it for presentation. The information is then sent via another superhighway to the video adapter, which translates it into television-type signals for the monitor. You don't have to keep track of which superhighway, called a *bus,* is involved in every operation, but it is important to understand that the various push-together connections you will make to the motherboard form vital bridges for the information flow.

Motherboards are not designed by manufacturers in a "reinventing the wheel" process. The design of the motherboard is largely controlled by the choice of the chipset; the one or two highly integrated chips that support the CPU. Although the CPU can be seen as the decision maker, it doesn't carry out the policing of all the motherboard superhighways (and back roads) by itself. The chipset handles all of the support functions for the motherboard, largely in automatic mode, just like the nervous system of the human body maintains our vital functions even while we sleep. The level of support offered by the chipset defines the capabilities that can be built into the motherboard, including what speeds will be possible for the CPU and memory. There are far fewer chipset manufacturers than motherboard manufacturers, and CPU manufacturers always design a companion chipset of their own to go with their CPUs.

Central Processing Unit (CPU)

The CPU is the brain of your PC, executing the instructions of the software programs you run, such as Windows XP, Linux, Word, and Quicken. Most PCs are referred to by their CPU and speed rating, such as a "3.4 GHz Pentium 4" or a "3800+ Athlon 64." Currently, all CPUs being manufactured for use in PCs run at speeds from a minimum of 1.8 gigahertz (GHz) to over 3 GHz, where hertz (Hz) expresses the number of clock cycles the CPU steps through in one second.

If you should ask, "What can a CPU do in a single step?" the answer is "It depends on the CPU." All CPUs can do several things at the same time, and the designers squeeze every drop of performance they can out of a clock cycle. Although it's no longer true that equivalent clock speeds for Intel and AMD CPUs express equivalent performance, the numbers are valid for comparing performance within a family of CPUs. Thus, a 3.2 GHz Pentium 4 can execute 33 percent more instructions/second than a 2.4 GHz Pentium 4. We'll talk more about how the speed of the CPU impacts the overall performance of the PC in the next chapter.

Figure 1.3
Intel Celeron CPU

One of the biggest bottlenecks to CPU performance is memory speed. These huge numbers for CPU speed we are casually throwing around don't mean much of anything unless the CPU can be supplied with instructions to carry out and data to operate on. To minimize the amount of time CPUs spend waiting for memory, small amounts of super-fast memory called *cache* are included in the CPU package. CPU manufacturers often use the amount of cache onboard to differentiate between high-priced chips destined for the server market and their desktop cousins. Depending on the type of work the CPU is doing, it might find as much as 90 percent of the data it is looking for in cache. Considering that the CPU cache is likely to amount to less than 1 percent of the total system memory, that's a pretty good hit rate.

System Memory or RAM

Random Access Memory (RAM) provides the fast, temporary storage from which your CPU draws the data it needs to operate. The storage capacity of RAM is measured in megabytes (millions of bytes). You'll want to build your new PC with an absolute minimum of 256 MB of RAM. If you are running very demanding applications or high data throughput jobs like video editing, you might want to install as much memory as you can afford. Currently, 512 MB is a pretty healthy amount, and is more than is included in most PCs sold in stores.

There are three basic families of RAM in use today, and we give an example of each with our three builds. The Dynamic RAM (DRAM) that makes up the system memory actually starts to forget everything many times a second, but a dedicated memory controller endlessly reads and writes this information to keep it fresh. Memory, amusingly enough, does forget everything the moment the PC is turned off, which is why we have hard drives, CDs, and floppies to provide storage. The fastest way to tip off a showroom vulture that you are a little hazy about computer terminology is to refer to "the memory in the hard drive."

Floppy Drives

Floppy drives have been around almost as long as the reel-to-reel tape drives that played such a big role in 1960s movies, in which the reels spinning back and forth showed that the computer was "thinking." The 1.44 MB floppy drive that is still standard in the majority of PCs has been around for about 18 years. Floppy drives once played a critical part in getting new PCs up and running, but this role has been replaced by bootable operating system CDs. The main function of floppy drives these days is to create emergency boot disks for virus removal software or undo disks for system utilities, like ScanDisk.

The 3.5" floppy disk in its hard plastic cartridge is still a convenient way to make a backup copy of your novel or your checkbook register, but due to their relatively low reliability, I keep more than one copy around. The actual recording media is a thin plastic disc with a magnetic coating on each side, and a protective coating on top. As with tape drives, the read/write head actually comes in contact with the media. Often, a floppy disk written in one PC will be unreadable in another due to poor manufacturing tolerances, so make sure you try reading your backup floppies in another PC before putting any great confidence in them.

Figure 1.4
Floppy drive

Hard Drives

The most important storage device in your PC is the hard drive. The average hard drive sold today can store as much information as fifty thousand or more floppy disks, and it can find and read that information faster than any other storage device, including CDs and DVDs. The majority of the storage space on most people's hard drive is used for programs, such as the operating system, word processing and database software, and games. No author, living or dead, could ever fill up a modern hard drive by writing books, but a few hours of uncompressed video would do the job. Although you can always make room on a nearly full hard drive by destroying (deleting) old programs or information, most people prefer to let the clutter build up like old boxes in the attic, simply adding a new hard drive when things get too crowded.

Although the storage provided by the hard drive is certainly permanent in comparison to RAM, it's nowhere near bulletproof. The mean time between failures (MTBF) ratings provided by hard drive manufacturers are highly optimistic, and often exceeds the useful life of the drive by at least a decade. Anecdotally, I would estimate that one in twenty hard drives suffers complete failure within a couple years of being purchased, with an even higher rate in notebook computers. These failures can result from all sorts of environmental issues, such as excessive heat, power spikes, or the PC getting thumped at just the wrong moment.

For this reason, anybody who uses the PC for more than games and Internet surfing should get in the habit of making copies of important information, a process known as "creating a backup." Creating a backup can be as simple as copying your checkbook register or word processing documents to a floppy disk once a week, but never use the floppy disks to exclusively store documents in place of the hard drive because they are far less reliable, not to mention much slower.

Figure 1.5
Inside the hard drive

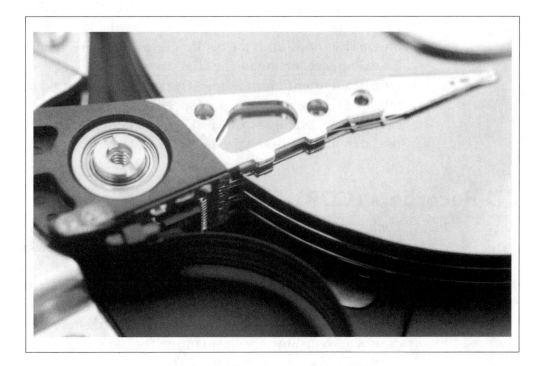

In critical business applications, a special technology called RAID (Redundant Array of Inexpensive Drives) provides a means to duplicate data across several hard drives to increase performance and protect against the failure of any individual drive. RAID solutions usually provide automatic failover, so you won't experience any downtime if a single drive fails in the middle of the business day. We will give two examples of simple RAID subsystems in our builds. In addition to the drive striping method that increases data integrity, RAIDs can also be used to increase performance or to create a giant storage volume.

However, RAID provides no protection against fire, theft, data management errors, or computer viruses. In fact, the only protection against fire and similar disasters is to store your backup copies in a remote location. Tape backups are the dominant device for backing up large amounts of data, although DVD recorders and new high-capacity cartridge drives from Iomega may pick up some of the load. CD recorders, also know as *burners,* provide an excellent option for data backup if you just organize your files on the hard drive so you know what to copy to the CD.

CD Drives

CDs were first developed by the music industry to compete with, and then replace, vinyl records. The CD drives in PCs are all capable of playing music CDs without the aid of any other hardware, and most come with a headphone jack right on the front of the drive. A CD holds a three mile–long spiral of information, where the location of a particular item is measured in minutes and seconds from the beginning, as if it were being played in a stereo. The difference among music CDs, data CDs, and all the various hybrids is strictly a matter of formatting. The speed at which your computer plays a music CD is fixed to be the same speed at which stereos play CDs, and this became known as single speed or 1X. The standard CD drives in use today can read data CDs at peak speeds of 50X or faster.

CD Recorders (CDR)

For less than $50 you can purchase a CDR drive that can record or play CDs. There are two varieties of CD blanks: the older type, which can be written once (CDR), and the newer type, which can be erased and rewritten many times (CDRW). All the production CDR drives can write to either type of blank, which is why the drives are labeled with three speeds: a write speed, a rewrite speed, and a read speed. Blank CDs of either type cost less than 20 cents when you buy them in quantity. The hard plastic CD holders, known as *jewel cases,* cost as much as the CDs do.

CD recorders are the best way invented yet of transferring large amounts of data between computers that aren't wired together on a fast network. The thing that makes CDs so ideal is that the standard was born outside the PC world, so any type of computer can read a data CD created in any other. The only trick is this: when you are recording music CDs to play in a stereo or data CDs as backups, use the write-only CDR media. The rewritable media (CDRW) is not compatible with all types of readers.

DVD Drives and Recorders

Digital Video Discs (DVDs) are another entertainment industry innovation, designed primarily to increase the quality of movies viewed at home and reduce the pirating that goes on with VHS tapes. DVDs held about as much information as seven CDs in their first incarnation, and about 28 times as much in their double-sided, double-layered version. DVD drives can read CDs, so there's no reason to put both types of disc readers in a new PC. Building a PC with a CDR for recording and a DVD for playing is a common compromise in low-cost PCs.

Figure 1.6
Dual format
Memorex DVD
recorder

Combination drives (CDR and DVD) are a little more expensive than CD recorders and a little cheaper than full DVD recorders. DVD recorders are now available for under $100, so many home PC builders will choose to include one. Unfortunately, the entertainment industry has yet to standardize on a single DVD format. One way to avoid getting stuck with a DVD recorder that could come out the loser in the standards battle is to buy a dual format drive. These drives can handle both of the popular formats, DVD +R and DVD -R, so if you encounter a DVD player that doesn't read both formats, you can still create DVDs for it. The +R and -R standards are sponsored by two competing industry groups, and the +R group was the first to achieve double layer recording, which doubles the potential capacity of discs from 4.7 GB to 9.4 GB. We built our Athlon 64 system with a double layer DVD recorder.

Tape Drives

Tape drives are still the number one solution for backing up business computer systems, although they never caught on in home PCs because of the cost and the unfriendly software. One problem with tape drives is that they are far from foolproof. Even professional network administrators sometimes fall into the trap of shuffling tapes each morning and assuming that the backup software is performing its job, only to find there is a problem with restoring the data when a disaster occurs. The danger is greatest when multiple tapes are introduced along with partial backups, in which the tape software only copies files that have changed since the last backup. The only way to make sure your backups are good is to do an occasional restore as a test.

Another problem with tape backups is you need a PC with a working tape drive and the proper tape software to recover files, as opposed to a CD, which can be read anywhere. Unlike all other storage media, which uses some variation of a rotating disk to allow any data to be positioned under the read head almost immediately, tapes need to be wound past the magnetic read head until the data is reached. Restoring a single small file from a tape usually takes several minutes, most of which the drive spends winding tape. Making a new complete backup of a hard drive can take several hours.

Modems

Modems give your home PC the capability to communicate with other computers over the phone lines or the cable and satellite TV infrastructure. For most people, this means connecting to the Internet or to a private corporate network. Other uses for modems include turning the PC into an answering machine, a fax machine, or a voice mail system, or for playing multiuser games.

Modems, compared with most of the other parts in your PC, are extremely slow. The standard telephone modem is capable of receiving 56 Kb/s (kilobits/second), one of the few times you'll see the puny "kilo" prefix in this book. Cable modems offer a substantial improvement over telephone modems, about a 50 fold increase in download speed under ideal conditions, but your local cable company might not provide the service or it might be too pricey.

There are a variety of advanced telephone modem technologies, the most popular of which is DSL (Digital Subscriber Line). These fall a little short of the ideal cable modem performance, but in the real world there isn't a whole lot of difference. Because cable bandwidth is shared within a neighborhood, your performance will drop if many neighbors install (and use) cable modems. DSL is not available everywhere, and even if you know people with DSL who use the same local phone company as you, you might be too far from the central phone office to get it yourself.

Figure I.7
56 Kb/s modem

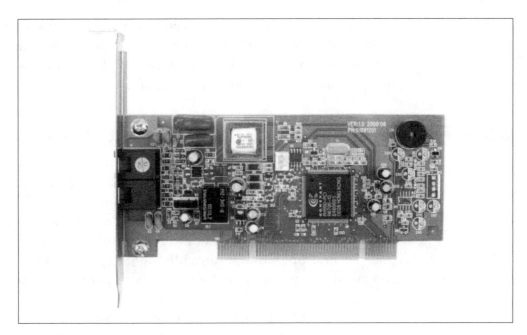

Figure I.7
56 Kb/s modem

Network Adapter

Everyone who works in an office environment is familiar with computer networks—or at least with computer networks being down. A network adapter in your PC plays essentially the same role as a modem, but it operates much, much faster. The standard network adapter operating at 100 Mb/s is almost two thousand times faster than the standard telephone modem operating at 56 Kb/s. Although many of the performance numbers tossed around for PCs have very little to do with the overall user experience, this one does. The standard network adapter can transfer more information in six seconds than a standard telephone modem can in three hours.

Network adapters are very inexpensive and are often included as a standard feature on the motherboard, and all of the current operating systems support networking without requiring a further investment in software. To set up a small home network, you need to buy a network *hub*, a combination of a switch box and a signal conditioner, in which the individual network cables running to the PCs are joined together. A small hub and a few cables will run you less than $75, allowing you to share files and printers. To share high-speed Internet access from the cable TV or the phone company, you'll need a router, which normally incorporates a small hub for around $100. Don't buy a router without first consulting with your high-speed Internet provider. They may insist on a particular brand or model, or even that you purchase the router from a particular store. You may want to include a network adapter in your PC even if you never plan to set up a network, in order to be cable modem ready. Wireless hubs and adapters are taking over the home networking environment as prices have fallen and installation doesn't require pulling cables or any special tools.

USB, FireWire, and I/O (Input/Output) Ports

In the early days of computing, there were three options for attaching peripherals to a PC. The first necessitated adding an expensive special adapter to the PC, such as a Small Computer Systems Interface (SCSI) card, which we'll talk about in the next chapter. The other two options were the standard printer port, and the two standard serial ports. The printer port has undergone several upgrades to provide higher speeds and enhanced two-way communications, allowing for a variety of peripherals to be attached.

The serial ports have fallen almost completely out of use, especially since the introduction of a separate mouse port. About the only peripherals still using serial ports are some early digital cameras, PDAs, and the rarely used external telephone modem. With the introduction of the home PC, a new type of I/O port was introduced for using a joystick to play computer games. The game port was once standard on sound cards or included in the motherboard I/O core if the motherboard had built-in sound.

As the number of high-speed, inexpensive devices available for attachment to the PC multiplied, an equally inexpensive way of attaching them was required. Universal Serial Bus (USB) is a true plug-and-play solution for attaching peripherals. You don't need to turn the PC off to attach or detach USB devices, and the software support in recent operating system releases is seamless. All modern joysticks and game controllers run off USB ports and game ports have all but disappeared from sound cards and motherboard I/O cores. However, there's often a connector on the motherboard where you can attach a cable to run a legacy game port through the back of the case.

All new motherboards come standard with two or more USB ports, and large numbers of USB devices can be connected to a single port using a USB hub. The single drawback with the first widely adopted USB standard (version 1.1) was that at maximum speed of 12 Mb/s, it wasn't fast enough to support many high-performance peripherals. That 12 Mb/s (megabits/second) translates into just 1.5 MB/s (megabytes/second), which is nowhere near fast enough to connect even the slowest external hard drives.

The early USB standard has been replaced by two competing technologies: FireWire and USB 2.0. FireWire (IEEE 1394) has been around for years, and has had great success in the multimedia storage markets. At a maximum speed of 400 Mb/s, it has more than enough bandwidth to keep the data moving, and it has the advantage of existing software support. USB 2.0 sports a maximum speed of 480 Mb/s, and backward compatibility with existing USB 1.1 devices. While both of these standards support external hard drives, the top theoretical speed will be less than half of that achievable with an external hard drive utilizing the brand new SATA (Serial ATA) technology discussed in the next chapter.

Figure 1.8
Adaptec USB 2.0 adapter

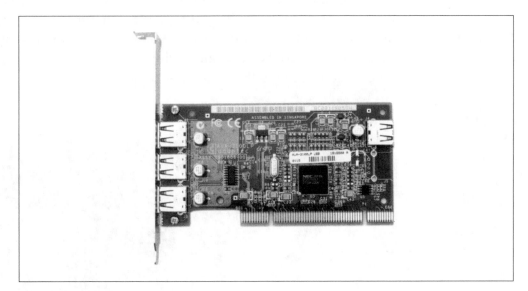

Sound Cards and Speakers

A sound card translates the digital data stored on your PC or downloaded from the Internet into the analog sounds waves you can hear, a process called Digital to Analog (D/A) conversion. Sound cards can also convert analog sound such as music or speech into digital data that can be stored or manipulated by the PC, a process called Analog to Digital (A/D) conversion. The primary features differentiating sound systems are the power and clarity of their amplifiers and speakers (that is, will your PC sound as good as your stereo?).

On a fixed budget, it makes more sense to buy a cheap sound card and expensive speakers. Marketing for sound cards once focused on their 3D effects, wave table sound, and polyphony capabilities. All these are relevant for musicians who will generate or mix music on their PCs, and for game players, but have nothing to do with how a music CD played on the PC will sound. *Wave table sound* allows the sound card to play a type of compressed music commonly used in games and multimedia presentations, in which the "true" waveform of the desired sound is formed from the wave table. *Polyphony* refers to how many independent sound streams the card can produce and mix at one instant.

These measures of performance have given way to Surround Sound support, necessary for the full theatre experience when playing DVD movies or compatible games. The lowest level of sound support these days is four-channel sound, front and back speaker pairs. Entry-level Surround Sound systems consist of front and back stereo, plus a back-center speaker and a subwoofer, abbreviated as 5.1 sound. Add front center speaker for 6.1 sound, or two side speakers for 7.1 sound. The six-speaker 5.1 Surround Sound setup is also known as six channel, and the 7.1 setup is known as eight channel. All of these sound channels won't add much to your experience unless you have reasonably high-quality speakers and movies or games that utilize them. To run PC sound into a true home entertainment system, most high-end sound solutions offer a Sony/Philips Digital Interface (S/PDIF) with options to connect by either a coax or optical cable.

Figure 1.9
PCI Surround
Sound 5.1 card

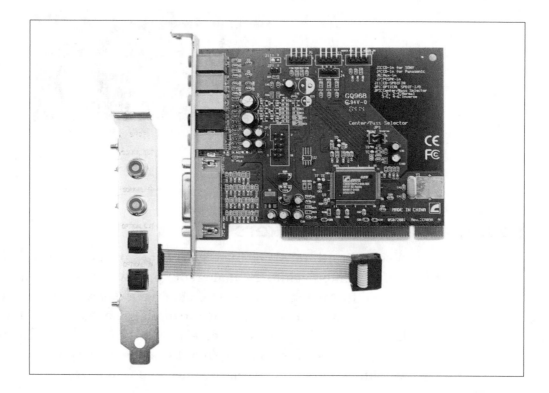

An up-and-coming use for sound cards in PC systems is for speech recognition. That is, talking to your PC. Speech recognition allows for hands-off operation of your computer, with dictation-to-type being the leading application. The technology is rapidly improving and finding acceptance with professionals in challenging environments such as medical and legal practices. Sound card capabilities are the most common candidate for integration on the motherboard, and two of the three PCs in this book required no sound adapter.

Keyboard and Mouse

Two of the cheapest peripherals attached to any computer are the keyboard and the mouse, which taken together can cost less than $20. If there is any correlation between the cost of keyboards and their quality, it's been my experience that the cheap keyboards last longer than the expensive ones. Mice, on the other hand, are generally a little nicer as you move up the price ladder, but all mechanical mice require the occasional cleaning. Cleaning the mouse is a five-minute job, usually undertaken when the mouse pointer on the screen insists on only moving up and down when you're trying to go left or right. Turn the mouse upside down, follow the direction arrow to pop off the ball retainer, and clean the lint off the two sets of rollers in the mouse. Keyboards are available in a variety of styles, from the 104/105 key rectangular keyboard to the split *V* keyboard and the oversize "surfer" keyboard with dedicated Internet keys.

Figure 1.10
Keyboard with Internet navigation buttons

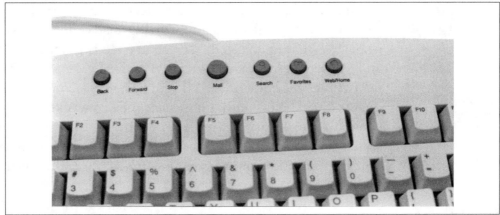

The Video Monitor

A large video monitor can be the most expensive component of a basic PC, which isn't such a bad thing because it's the only piece of hardware other than the printer that comes anywhere near holding its value over time. A monitor is similar to an artist's canvas in that it presents no images or information on its own. It needs to be painted by a remote hand; in this case, the video adapter. The video adapter installed in your PC might cost only 20 percent as much as the monitor, yet it controls the resolution and the number of colors displayed.

The vast majority of today's monitors are based on one of two competing technologies: cathode-ray tubes (CRTs) or liquid crystal displays (LCDs). While CRT monitors have dominated the market since the original introduction of the PC, the LCD technology that made laptop and notebook computers possible is winning an increasing share of the desktop space.

CRT Monitors

Monitors, like televisions, are described by the diagonal measurement of the picture tube, in inches. All things being equal, when a 17" monitor displays the same image as a 14" monitor, the picture or text is nearly 50 percent larger. However, the true viewable area of a monitor rarely reaches the actual picture tube measurements, depending on how much of the tube is covered by the plastic housing and whether or not the monitor controls allow you to adjust the picture out to the edges. A basic understanding of the internal workings of a monitor is nice to have, but if you are buying inexpensive components, you don't need to worry about it.

The data to be displayed on the monitor screen is first converted from digital to analog form (from bits to waves) by the video adapter. These waves use varying voltage levels to describe the intensity for red, green, and blue electron guns to fire in order to paint each point on the display, along with a synchronizing signal. The monitor electronics steer the beams from these electron guns by use of magnetic fields (also called *lenses*), which deflect the beams down and across the screen at speeds determined by the horizontal and vertical refresh frequencies. The vertical refresh rate describes how many times the entire screen is redrawn in a second, and the horizontal frequency must be fast enough to steer the beam all the way across the screen enough times to paint every *pixel* (point on the screen) in a single vertical scan. These refresh frequencies are included in the product information sheet for every monitor, and the higher numbers usually mean better quality.

Figure 1.11
17" monitor displaying two pages of text

Pixels provide a measure of image resolution (detail), with no dependence on the monitor used. A picture made up from a grid of 640 horizontal points and 480 vertical points (640 × 480) is the lowest quality image (plain VGA) used on computers today, and even this is appreciably sharper than a standard TV picture. Even the least expensive monitors used today can display much higher resolution (finer) images than this, but for many people, an inexpensive monitor flickers noticeably when pushed to the higher resolutions. The main factor controlling monitor flicker is the vertical refresh rate, and a monitor capable of 75–85 redraws per second (75 Hz or higher) at a given resolution will produce a really solid picture.

The sharpness of the images painted is dependent on the *dot pitch* or *stripe pitch* of the monitor phosphor. The *pitch* is a measure, in millimeters, of the distance between two phosphor dots or stripes of the same color on the inside surface of the monitor screen. Some manufacturers use an aperture or mask pitch measurement that describes the size of the holes in part of the beam focusing train, but an equivalent dot pitch measurement should be available. Likewise, LCD screens give an equivalent dot pitch number, although no electron beams or phosphor is involved. The smaller the dot pitch, the finer the image, although there might be a trade-off in brightness. CRTs do have a few advantages over LCDs, primarily their wide viewing angle, their capability to display high-speed motion without blurring, and their superior flexibility in displaying high resolutions.

LCD Monitors

Most PC builders would choose a LCD monitor over a CRT without a second thought if not for the price difference. LCD monitors currently cost three to five times as much as CRTs for the same screen size as their bulky alternative. Some of the native advantages of LCD monitors are their low weight and power consumption, not to mention the small footprint that saves several square feet of space on the desktop.

Every pixel on an LCD monitor is a physically unique unit comprised of three LCD cells called *subpixels*. The subpixels allow light generated behind the cell to pass through the color filter in front of the cell, where the brightness is dependent on the amount of light passed through the liquid crystal, which is controlled by the applied voltage. The color filter in front of each pixel consists of Red, Green and Blue elements, one color over each subpixel. The final color and brightness of each unique pixel on the screen is a blend of the light passed through each of the subpixel filters, just like the color of each CRT pixel is determined by a blend of the luminescence of the three phosphor colors. The top resolution of the LCD monitor is limited to the total number of pixel units, as low as 800 × 600 on less expensive units.

Video Adapters

The Advanced Graphics Port (AGP) adapters that have ruled the roost for the past five years are finally seeing competition from the arrival of PCI Express. The main figure of merit for these adapters is the amount of video RAM they sport and the speed of the special purpose video signal processor. Current AGP adapters also have a basic speed rating of 4X or 8X, which describes the maximum data transfer rate they can achieve in ideal circumstances compared to the original AGP speed which is defined as 1X. PCI Express adapters were just being introduced as this book was published, but they promise to eventually boost speed to several times that of today's AGP adapters.

You can spend a lot of money on a video adapter for rapidly rendering high-resolution 3D images for animation. These adapters find their primary applications in heavy imaging environments in which the product is the picture, such as medical imaging, multimedia production, and of course, games. For most home users, the standard $50 AGP adapter is more than adequate, and in some cases, less prone to compatibility problems than adapters costing ten times as much. A popular feature on many video cards is a television tuner, which effectively turns your PC into a TV.

Figure 1.12
8X AGP video adapter with 128 MB RAM

Many new motherboards come with *onboard* video, an AGP adapter and connection port integrated into the motherboard, which eliminates the need for an add-in adapter. Surprisingly, these motherboards often cost less than similar motherboards without video capabilities. Motherboards with integrated video are frequently used by mass manufacturers, but are rarely chosen by home PC builders for three reasons:

1. The capabilities of the integrated video controller are often limited in comparison to even the most inexpensive video adapters.

2. The video adapter shares the main memory on the motherboard with the system. This means if you have a limited amount of memory installed, you are giving some of it up to the video controller.

3. Manufacturers of motherboards with an integrated AGP controller don't include an AGP slot for an add-in adapter. Therefore, if the onboard video controller is too slow or fails, you can't replace it with a standard AGP adapter; you'll have to fall back on an older PCI (Peripheral Component Interface) model.

Operating Systems

For most PC builders, the choice of operating system is similar to Henry Ford's famous Model T quote, "You can get it in any color, as long as it's black." For those who want to run all the shrink-wrapped software and games sold in stores, you can run any operating system as long as it's Microsoft Windows. The current version is Windows XP, available in both home and business versions, but some people will prefer to install the older versions with which they are familiar, such as Me, 2000, NT, 98, or even 95. The standard bearer of the "Anybody but Microsoft" movement continues to be the freeware Linux operating system, but its market penetration is largely limited to servers and techies. There are hundreds of excellent freeware applications that run under Linux, but don't expect to see it listed on the side of the Microsoft Office box any time soon.

Unit Shorthand	Unit Written Out	Actual Value	Applies To	Nominal Range
b	Bit	0 or 1, expressed as a voltage level	Bus width, memory module width	8, 16, 32, 64, 128, 256
B	Byte	8 bits, an unsigned number between 0 and 255	Basic unit of capacity	Byte, kilobyte, megabyte, gigabyte
KB	Kilobyte	1,000 bytes (rounded from 1,024)	File size	1 KB to many MBs
MB	Megabyte	1 million bytes	Capacity for memory modules, CDs, floppies	1 MB–1 GB
GB	Gigabyte	1 billion bytes	Capacity, hard drives, DVDs	1 GB to terabytes
Kb/s	Kilobits/second	1,000 bits per second	Modem and I/O port speeds	9,600–768 Kb/s
Mb/s	Megabits/second	1 million bits per second	Network and serial bus transfer speeds	10–480 Mb/s
KB/s	Kilobytes/second	1,000 bytes per second	File download speed via Internet	1–100 KB/s
MB/s	Megabytes/second	1 million bytes per second	Bus (SCSI, IDE, PCI, AGP) transfer speed	3–1,066 MB/s
MHz	Megahertz	1 million cycles per second	CPU clock, bus clock	33–1,000 MHz
GHz	Gigahertz	1 billion cycles per second	CPU clock	1–4 GHz
ms	Milliseconds	1/1000 of a second	Drive seek time, keyboard repeat rate	5–300 ms
ns	Nanoseconds	1 billionth of a second	Memory access time	6–70 ns
d	Dot	A unique point	Computer screens	0.25–0.31mm (as in dot pitch of screen)
dpi	Dots per inch	Dots printed or scanned from a linear inch	Printers, scanner	100–2,400 dpi
$	Dollars	100 cents	All PC components	$5 for a mouse to hundreds for high-end parts

Chapter 2

Selecting and Purchasing Parts

In this chapter, we will review the basic component choices you need to make before you begin purchasing parts. If you have some experience with assembling PCs, the relationships between these parts will already be clear to you. If not, we suggest you take some time now to browse through the assembly photographs in Chapters 4 through 6 to see how PCs are put together. This will give you a little familiarity with the physical appearance of the parts, along with the sizing relationships and connections that will be made between the components. We introduce the subject of shopping for parts before selecting them, because finding good pricing has a lot to do with which parts you can afford to select.

There are two major sources for buying computer parts at good prices, and each has its advantages and disadvantages. The first source is mail order, based on print advertisements or Internet sites. The main advantages of mail order are price, unlimited selection, and the security inherent in credit card transactions. The hidden time bomb of mail order purchasing is shipping costs and turnaround time, both the initial cost to get the parts to you and any reshipping costs and delays due to mistakes or defective merchandise.

One way to minimize shipping costs is to buy all your parts from the same mail-order supplier. However, you must clearly state at the time of your order that you will not accept partial shipment, or the delivery charges could start mounting up. Even worse, your order might show up lacking some critical component that could be another week in coming, effectively postponing the build. In extreme cases, partial shipments may be accepted and paid for, only for the supplier to e-mail two weeks later and inform you they no longer stock the missing part at all. Some mail order outfits charge fixed shipping amounts per component, and a $5 shipping charge for a $5 network card or modem is the same as doubling the price. When you do comparative shopping online, make sure that you include the exact shipping and handling charges, or you may end up paying more than if you bought from a site with higher list prices. Another problem with some mail order outlets is that the prices you are quoted may mysteriously creep up a few bucks here and there. This will generally be attributed to "a problem in the system," but by reading your invoice and complaining to your credit card company, you can be sure to pay what you intended.

The other source for reasonably priced computer parts is retail computer stores and superstore chains. The superstores have the advantage of volume buying power, particularly on boxed items that move quickly such as printers, monitors, scanners, and drives. Manufacturer and store rebates are another way to lower your component cost at superstores, and on the whole, rebate fulfillment has improved over the last five years or so. Still, it pays to make a photocopy of the rebate paperwork in case it falls between the cracks.

The friendly neighborhood computer shop is a much better source for advice, and will probably carry a greater variety of CPUs, motherboards, and cases. The neighborhood shop will also be able to order any special parts for you, although not as cheaply as you could get them through direct mail order. The main advantage of retail stores is that if you get a defective part, you can pop back in and return it for another one, usually hassle free. You can't expect to get a good deal on all your parts in a retail store. They are particularly bad on items such as memory, video adapters, and cables, but they often sell hard drives and DVDRs as loss leaders to get you in the door.

Computer shows were once a major source of parts, combining mail order pricing with retail availability. In fact, the vendor pricing at some shows was so aggressive that you had to wonder if their merchandise fell off a truck. Aside from pricing, the main advantage of shows was you could really get your hands on the parts you were buying. Often the vendor would have an open PC at the table to stick the parts in and prove they were working. They also handed out plenty of free advice about what you wanted and why, and you could see a lot of things you would buy if money were no object.

However, the popularity of these shows has died down with the maturity of the industry, and there were several problems associated with them. One drawback was that the cost for a fly-by-night outfit to set up a booth at a computer show for the weekend was appreciably less than the cost of an ad in a magazine. This meant that anybody with $100 in his pocket could set up a

"Moe's Computer" sign, sell you stuff with a three-year warranty, and then disappear off the face of the earth on Monday morning. Another drawback was the frenetic show atmosphere that can lead to hasty purchasing decisions and leave shoppers vulnerable to high-pressure sales tactics.

Monitors, printers, and other peripherals should be purchased locally whenever possible. The shipping costs for these often exceed $30, depending on your location, and you should be able to get a decent deal at the local office superstore or computer chain store. There are search engines on the Internet specifically geared toward helping you shop for parts. The most popular is probably Pricewatch (www.pricewatch.com), but you can also try www.streetprices.com or www.salescircular.com for weekly sales at electronics discounters and office supply chains.

A system including a case, power supply, motherboard, memory, CPU, and video card is generally referred to as a "bare bones system." Even without any drives or other adapters installed, you can attach a monitor to a bare bones system and get a live screen. There are big advantages to buying the bare bones of your system from a single source. First of all, that supplier should accept responsibility that the components you have chosen will work together when assembled properly. This means you won't end up with a CPU not supported by your motherboard, or the wrong voltage AGP video adapter. Another advantage is that if you have difficulty getting your assembled system to work, your vendor can't try to shift the blame to other suppliers.

Paying for Performance

To do full justice to all of the new technologies and variations that are used in today's PCs, we would have to triple or quadruple the number of pages in this book, and then you would have to sift through them! Our compromise is to supply enough information to enable you to make educated buying decisions for parts, without trying to invade the turf of PC magazines, whose primary mission is to provide reviews of the latest and greatest hardware. There are also some excellent web sites that post daily reviews of PC components, most notably Tom's Hardware Guide (www.tomshardware.com), Anand Tech (www.anandtech.com), and Sharky Extreme (www.sharkyextreme.com).

You don't need to master all the terms and technology in this chapter to build a PC. In fact, the actual assembly job requires very little knowledge about the technology and performance of the individual parts. Good vendors can help you choose the right combination of components to meet your performance needs and budget, but beware that they will interpret "meeting the budget" as "spending all the money allotted." No book can make you a purchasing expert until you get some hands-on experience, but hopefully the information in this chapter will help you ask the right questions before you lay out your hard-earned cash. The toughest question you must ask yourself when purchasing parts for your PC is, "How much performance do I need today?" There is no point in trying to cover any possible future needs with what you buy today, particularly since you are building your own PC and can easily upgrade it a year from now when that $600 CPU you were looking at costs less than $200. The capacities and performance of most standard computer parts sold today far exceed the average demand. For example, the majority of PCs currently in use have hard drives smaller than 40 GB, and most people never fill these up. Yet, the average hard drive sold today has a capacity of 80 GB or more and costs less than 10 GB drives cost when they were popular a couple years ago. If you plan to record a lot of video and music or store thousands of high-resolution images, by all means, buy the largest hard drive on the market. If not, buy the 40 GB drive with the rebate for less than $50.

The dirty little secret of the PC industry is that performance increases are rarely cumulative. In other words, if you select five components (a CPU, a hard drive, a DVD recorder, a video adapter, and RAM), each of which guarantees you a 20 percent increase in performance over the lower priced versions of the same, you won't end up with a PC that's 100 percent faster. You're more likely to end up with a PC that's 20 percent faster, some of the time. Why not all the time? Well, if you spend a lot of time surfing the Web, the pages aren't going to load any faster. The limiting factor there is the 56 Kb/s modem, and a slow computer with a cable or DSL modem will blow the doors off a fast computer with an old telephone modem when it comes to Web surfing. If you print a lot of color pictures on your inkjet, they won't print any faster. The real bottleneck here is the printer itself. What is cumulative about the five "high-performance" parts is the price. That hypothetical PC will cost twice as much. In fact, unless you are an avid game player pushing motion 3D graphics to their limit, your PC spends most of its time waiting for you to ask it to do something.

Selecting a CPU

In the first chapter we introduced cases, power supplies, and motherboards before CPUs, because without these, the CPU is helpless. However, when it comes to purchasing the parts to build a system, the choice of CPU controls which motherboard, power supply, and memory you will require. There are two real players in the CPU manufacturing game: Intel and Advanced Micro Devices (AMD). Intel retains the lion's share of the market, especially in the business world where brand recognition is king, but AMD is steadily gaining in popularity with home PC builders and gamers.

Intel's flagship processor in the consumer PC market still carried the Pentium 4 name at press time, though the newer versions differ greatly from the original. The latest version of the Pentium 4 utilizes Socket 775 and has abandoned the Pin Grid Array (PGA) that characterized CPU package designs for the past five years in favor of a Land Grid Array (LGA). The PGA design made the electrical connection between the CPU and the motherboard through a dense grid of pins, or legs, protruding from the bottom of the CPU package. The LGA design moves the grid of pins to the socket, with mere landing pads remaining on the CPU package. The AMD Athlon 64 compares well with the fastest Pentium 4s in most applications, despite the Pentium 4's higher clock speeds. AMD's 32-bit Athlon XP and Duron chips designed for Socket A offer capable, low-cost alternatives for limited budgets, as does the Intel Celeron or earlier versions of the Pentium 4 in Socket 478. AMD recently introduced the Sempron processor, which will replace the Duron name as the economical processor. All modern CPUs require an active *heatsink,* a metal finned structure for radiating heat topped by a cooling fan.

Figure 2.1
Installing a Socket A heatsink

CPU prices are structured to take advantage of business buyers for whom a few hundred dollars in cost difference is a small factor in the overall purchasing decision. Never buy the fastest speed CPU within a family of processors, or you'll be paying a couple hundred dollars extra for a speed difference that is impossible to detect in most applications. If you have the extra money to spend, consider using it on options with far more impact, like a large monitor, better printer or video adapter, more memory, or a high-speed Internet connection. One of the best reasons for building your own PC is that you can maximize your value without getting stuck paying for the fastest CPU and other parts you don't need. CPUs should not be chosen for their internal architectural design features, which are entirely transparent to the user. Terms like "super scalar," "super pipelined," "multiple branch prediction," and "out-of-order processing" apply to all the current CPU designs and do not offer a rational basis for comparison. All the CPUs used in this book are fully x86-compatible (they will work with software written for any PC since the IBM AT) and support the industry standard MMX (MultiMedia eXtension) instructions. This means they will be capable of running any shrink-wrapped PC software you might buy.

There are four factors to take into consideration when choosing a CPU: the price, the speed rating, the memory support, and the suitability of compatible motherboards. The speed of a CPU in GHz is really only relevant when comparing it to an identical CPU at a different speed. Although higher numbers always mean faster, the overall performance gain of the PC as measured by the user's experience comes nowhere near reflecting the increased speed rating. Different versions of the same CPU can require entirely different memory technologies, or support them at different levels of performance. Motherboards for older CPUs are always much cheaper than those for the latest models. A recently released, top-speed CPU and motherboard can cost as much as $1000 together, while a previous generation CPU and motherboard capable of running Windows XP just fine will cost less than $200. Both Intel and AMD have run into physical limits in ramping up the clock speeds of their CPUs, with heat dissipation being a primary cause. AMD dropped out of the raw clock speed race first, but kept up with Intel CPU performance through innovations in processor design. Both manufacturers have now turned to improving the CPU interfacing with the memory and the video adapter as ways to increase performance without running up the actual clock speed. AMD and Intel have both announced plans for next-generation dual-core CPUs that will essentially provide multiprocessor performance on a single chip.

Intel Pentium 4 for Socket 775

Identifying a CPU by name without having to write a short essay has become increasingly difficult, as manufacturers have retained the same basic brand names for years and differentiated the products through a list of their characteristics. Intel CPUs are frequently identified through the code names assigned to the processor or supporting chipset during the development phases, like "Alderwood," "Prescott," "Grantsdale," and so forth. The problem is that these names rarely survive in the marketplace once full-scale production is reached, and buyers and sellers alike are left talking about the

CPUs in terms of their Front Side Bus (FSB) support and the CPU socket. For the sake of this discussion, I'm differentiating between the most recent Pentium 4s and the last generation by the CPU socket. The first build in our book is a Pentium 4 in Socket 775 with an 800 MHz FSB, PCI Express video, and DDR2-533 memory. The retail package designation of the CPU is the Pentium 4 560.

Figure 2.2
Socket 775 LGA

AMD Athlon 64 in Socket 939

The second build in our book is an AMD Athlon 64 3800+ with 8X AGP and dual-channel DDR400 memory. The Athlon 64 is the first fully backward-compatible 64-bit CPU for desktop computing, meaning it runs all the existing 32-bit software seamlessly. The Athlon 64 was originally released for Socket 754, and these motherboards are still widely available, but we build our system in Socket 939, which will be the primary platform by 2005. The early versions of the Athlon 64 FX chips for gaming started in Socket 940, before moving to Socket 939. The 64-bit AMD CPUs will be able to take full advantage of their larger registers and address bus when Microsoft releases a final version of Windows XP for 64-bit CPUs. A 32-bit version of the low-cost Sempron processor is available for Socket 754 and is expected for Socket 939 in 2005.

Intel Pentium 4 and Celeron for Socket 478

The third build in our book is an Intel Pentium 4 in Socket 478 motherboard, also from Intel. This is the only build we do with RAMBUS technology (more on memory later in this chapter). The original Pentium 4 was designed for Socket

423, which is appreciably larger than the newer Socket 478. You cannot mount a Socket 423 Pentium 4 on a Socket 478 motherboard or vice versa, and Socket 423 has disappeared from the marketplace. This shrinking of the socket and the CPU package is made possible by continual advancements in the semiconductor technology, primarily reductions in the actual size of the microscopic transistors on the chip. Intel has also been a leader in developing new heatsinks for CPUs, improving not only performance, but also ease of installation on.

Figure 2.3
Intel Pentium 4
and Socket 478

AMD Athlon XP and Duron for Socket A

The Athlon XP and the Duron for Socket A (also known as Socket 462) are identical in appearance, and utilize the same heatsink. The real difference between the Athlon and the Duron, aside from the clock speeds available, is the amount of cache memory on the processor. Beginning with the Athlon XP, AMD established a new performance rating for CPUs, based on benchmark performance rather than the clock speed in gigahertz or megahertz. These new performance ratings offer an equivalent megahertz rating followed by a "+". The Socket A CPUs will remain available for a while if there's market demand, and AMD just released the new Sempron CPU for Socket A. Readers may refer to the Third Edition of *Build Your Own PC* for a full Socket A build.

Multiprocessor and Workstation CPUs

Given an infinite amount of money, one way to get more performance out of a computer is to put multiple CPUs on a special motherboard and to run software designed to take advantage of them. AMD's 64-bit Opteron pro cessors are available for multiprocessor configurations, initially in Socket 940, but are now migrating to Socket 939, along with the consumer Athlon 64 FX, which is based on the Opteron core. The Pentium 4 has always been sup ported in multiprocessor configurations, and the Athlon MP is AMD's 32-bit multiprocessor solution for Socket A. Intel has further differentiated the market between PCs and servers with their line of Xeon processors, en hanced versions of the Pentium series CPUs that were priced out of the home PC market. In the 64-bit realm, Intel's Itanium processors are aimed squarely at the high-end server and workstation market, but have failed to make great headway due to their lack of backward compatibility.

CPU	Package Types Currently Available	Speeds Currently Available[1]	FSB Speed[2]	Basic Price/Top Performance Price
Intel Pentium 4 LGA	Socket 775	>2.8 GHz	800 MHz	$180/$500
AMD Athlon 64 AMD Athlon 64 FX	Socket 939 Socket 754 Socket 939 Socket 940	>2.8 GHz+	2 GHz (Memory controller integrated)	$170/$700 $600/$800
Intel Pentium 4 Intel Celeron D Intel Celeron	Socket 478	>1.7 GHz >2.4 GHz >1.4 GHz	400 MHz to 800 MHz, depends on model	$100/$400 $70/$130 $35/$85
AMD Sempron	Socket A, Socket 754 and Socket 939 expected	>2.2 GHz+	166 MHz / 333 MHz for Socket A	$40/$125
AMD Athlon XP AMD Duron	Socket A Socket A	>1.5 GHz+ >800 MHz	200 MHz to 400 MHz, depends on model	$40/$140 $25/$45

1. *The CPUs are available at the speed following the > and higher. Earlier generations of the same CPU may have been available at lower*
   speeds. The + following AMD ratings indicates an equivalent performance measure, not the actual clock speed.
2. *FSB speed reflects current models on the market.*

Motherboards

The CPU and the motherboard are so interdependent that it's a little unfair to have to put one before the other. As we mentioned earlier, you really should n't pick a CPU without considering the motherboard price and peripheral support in the overall picture. New motherboards support the latest CPUs, memory technologies, and interfaces for drives and peripherals. Mother boards that support the older CPUs tend to be loaded with more extras, such as integrated modems and video, than newer motherboards. One reason is that manufacturers in a mature market need to add features to compete. An other reason is that older CPUs are destined for lower-end systems in which cost takes precedence over performance. Mail order outfits that specialize in motherboard sales always offer a wide variety of motherboards, each with a list of price points for the different speeds of CPUs the board supports. In other words, they consider a CPU to be a motherboard option, and there is a lot of logic in their approach.

The main differentiation between motherboards is their CPU support. Although this information is given in the preceding table, we'll run through it quickly one more time. Socket 775 supports the latest Pentium 4 CPUs in the LGA (no pins) package. Socket 939 and Socket 754 motherboards support the two basic Athlon 64 versions. Socket 940 was initially used with the Athlon 64 FX and Opteron, but is being replaced by Socket 939 in the consumer market. Socket 478 motherboards support earlier Pentium 4 CPUs and Celerons, while the very early Socket 423 motherboards and CPUs are obsolete. Socket A motherboards support Athlons and Durons. For a quick trip down memory lane, Socket 370 motherboards supported Pentium III and Celeron CPUs, and Slot 1 motherboards support the older, cartridge-style Pentium IIIs (and older Celerons and Pentium IIs), which were built in the previous edition of this book. So, given a variety of motherboards that support the particular CPU you have chosen, the job is to look at the other motherboard features (including price) and pick one.

Figure 2.4
Selecting
FSB speed on
Athlon/Duron
motherboard

The choice of CPU and motherboard will determine which of the three current memory technologies you can use. Whatever memory technology your motherboard uses, make sure it supports dual-channel memory if you're building for performance. In all cases, the number of memory modules that can be installed and the total amount of memory supported will vary from motherboard to motherboard, but with memory prices as cheap as they are, the capability to upgrade memory by adding more later has become relatively unimportant. Some of the very latest motherboards allow previously unavailable flexibility in mixing memory modules, even allowing different-sized modules to be used in odd-numbered amounts for dual-channel operation.

Drive support is another component to consider when choosing a motherboard, now that the industry is transitioning from the old IDE (parallel ATA) drives to serial ATA. Most motherboards will continue to support the old IDE interfaces for some time because the performance offered by SATA simply isn't required for optical drives, like CDs and DVDs, and optical drives with SATA connectors have been slow to appear. Most new motherboards also support some level of drive arrays, which previously required an expensive add-in adapter.

An integrated network adapter is a great feature, but I wouldn't put too much faith in motherboard modems. You're usually better off with an add-in fax/modem adapter. All motherboards come stock with two serial I/O ports and one parallel (printer port), abbreviated 2S/1P, and two USB ports, not to mention PS/2-style keyboard and mouse ports. Newer motherboards often include a FireWire port, four or more USB 2.0 ports, and full Surround Sound (5.1 sound). These ports are mounted on the back edge of the motherboard, known as the *I/O core*. Today's computer cases normally ship with a universal I/O shield on the back of the case that has punch-out blanks to fit a basic motherboard's I/O core features. Motherboards with nonstandard I/O cores will ship with a custom I/O shield that can be snapped into place.

If you aren't buying a super-integrated motherboard with a large number of integrated features, you'll want a number of expansion slots for add-in adapters. Highly integrated motherboards are often extremely stingy with bus slots. There are three types of bus slots for add-in adapters on modern motherboards, the oldest of which is the venerable Peripheral Connect Interface (PCI). The most common implementation of PCI, sometimes called "Conventional PCI," is a 32-bit bidirectional interface that operates at a speed of 33 MHz in most consumer PCs. This results in a bandwidth of 133 MB/s, which is more than sufficient for add-in cards like modems and sound cards, but can barely keep up with a Gigabit Ethernet card (125 MB/s), which would swamp all of the available capacity. PCI is nowhere near fast enough for modern graphics adapters, which led to the introduction of a single Advanced Graphics Port (AGP) per motherboard, which doubled the top PCI performance in its first implementation. Some years later, AGP appears to have maxed out at 8X its original speed and will be slowly pushed aside by PCI Express 16X. PCI Express is a serial bus that uses low-voltage differential pairs for each transmission direction. All four available speeds for PCI Express were introduced simultaneously, with the 1X version (one pair in each direction) outstripping PCI by a factor of 15, and the 16X version doubling performance of the fastest AGP bus. Because the performance of PCI Express so far outstrips the needs of most add-in adapters, it will probably take a while for PCI modems and other adapters to make the conversion.

In addition to a single high-speed video adapter slot, motherboards also feature a number of conventional PCI slots, and you may be able to find a special motherboard with an ancient ISA slot if you really need to carry over a legacy adapter from a ten-year-old PC. Motherboards with PCI Express 16X video will also feature a couple PCI Express 8X, 4X, or 1X slots, usually in combination with some conventional PCI slots. It's a little hard to predict what adapters will require the performance that 4X or 8X PCI Express bus slots offer, probably the next-generation 10 Gigabit network cards, perhaps some new multimedia adapters.

Keep an eye on the PCI standard supported. The 2.2 version dominated for years, and supported newer 3.3V and older 5.0V adapters, but the 2.4 standard abandons backward compatibility. PCI adapters and slots are keyed so you shouldn't be able to force an old adapter into a slot that won't support it.

Figure 2.5
PCI slots

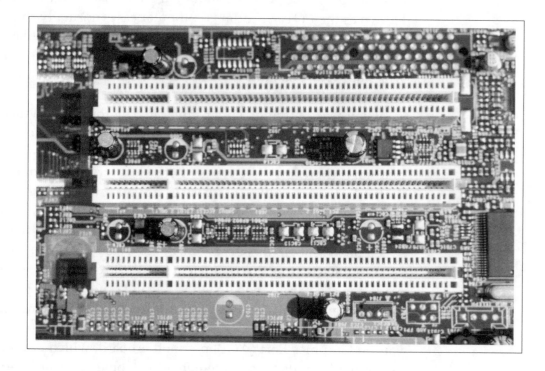

Motherboard Brand	CPU Support	Features[1]	Price
Intel D925XCV	Pentium 4 LGA 775	Dual Channel DDR2, PCI Express 16X, 7.1 Sound, Gigabit LAN	$190
Abit AS8	Pentium 4 LGA 775	Dual Channel DDR, 8X AGP, 10/100 LAN, 5 PCI slots	$130
ASUS A8v	Athlon 64 / 64FX in Socket 939	Dual Channel DDR, 8X AGP, Gigabit LAN, 5.1 Sound	$130
FIC K8 800T	Athlon 64 in Socket 754	Single Channel DDR, 8X AGP, Firewire	$75
Intel D845HV	Pentium 4 or Celeron in Socket 478 (2.6 GHz max)	PC133 SDRAM, 4X AGP, 10/100 LAN, 4 USB	$30
MSI MS6380	Athlon XP or Duron in Socket A	DDR, 4X AGP, IDE RAID	$25

1. *Features listing is partial and selective.*

Memory

We try to avoid giving history lectures in this book, but on the subject of memory, a brief review is essential to understanding the terminology. One of the basic innovations that made digital computers practical, Random Access Memory (RAM) allows the CPU to retrieve information stored at a specific memory address without having to read through all the memory to find it. Contrast this with a tape drive, where the whole tape may have to be wound by the read head to reach the location of the desired information. Even with the relatively fast hard drive, the read head must physically move, as much as hundreds of millimeters, and wait for the disk to spin until the information is under the head.

The access times of drives are measure in *milliseconds,* or thousandths of a second; the access time of RAM is measured in *nanoseconds,* or billionths of a second. When it comes to locating a single byte of data at a random location, memory outperforms other storage media by a factor of hundreds of thousands. If this wasn't the case, the super-fast CPUs would have no purpose, because they would spend all their time waiting for new instructions and for data to work on.

There are two basic types of RAM in use in PCs: Static RAM (SRAM) and Dynamic RAM (DRAM). Both types of memory forget everything if the power is turned off, but SRAM doesn't require the constant refreshing the DRAM does, ergo the names, "Static" and "Dynamic." SRAM requires four or five times as many transistors to implement as DRAM, as it traps each bit of information in a structure called a *flip-flop.* DRAM stores a bit as a temporary charge on the leg of a single transistor, but this decays away so rapidly that it must be reread and refreshed many times per second. SRAM is used as cache memory on CPUs and in other applications, but always in relatively small amounts, due to its increased power and real estate demands. DRAM is used for the main PC memory, and has been since the original IBM PC was introduced over 20 years ago. Flash RAM, a truly nonvolatile memory technology (maintains data without power), is widely used in peripherals such as digital cameras and key-chain storage devices.

Fast Page Memory (FPM) was the first big performance enhancement to DRAM, which had previously treated each new memory transaction like a surprise invitation. FPM made it faster to access data in the same memory "page," although the term "row" offers a better representation of what really goes on. When a new data bit is to come from the same matrix row as the previous bit, the memory controller needs only to increment the column location and the same row address will be used, saving an address transaction.

Extended Data Out (EDO) DRAM shortened the recovery time between sequential DRAM reads, offering about a 20 percent performance boost in overall memory throughput. EDO was backward compatible, meaning it would function in systems that were designed to support FPM RAM, albeit without any performance increase. Burst EDO (BEDO) was the next level of enhancement in which a series, or burst, of bytes from memory could be transferred to the CPU in a single request. If the CPU actually required data from these subsequent locations, an operation has been saved, and if not, nothing has been lost.

Synchronous DRAM (SDRAM) really boosted memory bandwidth through synchronization with the system clock. This eliminates a large number of timing delays, which can result in wait states on the part of the CPU (that is, idle time). Motherboards designed to support SDRAM were not backward compatible to EDO or FPM. Early SDRAM modules were 5V devices, but the later modules required 3.3V. Fortunately, memory module designers got together early on and came up with a standard system of notches in the contact edge of memory modules, which prevents them from being installed in the wrong type of memory socket. SDRAM was originally available at 66 MHz, but 100 MHz (PC100) and 133 MHz (PC133) devices soon followed. Basic SDRAM development topped out around PC150 (150 MHz) and was popular with overclockers.

Double Data Rate (DDR) SDRAM, simply known as DDR, is the next step after SDRAM. DDR can effectively double the throughput of earlier SDRAMs by transferring data on both the rising and falling edges of the bus clock. The original 32-bit Athlon was the first CPU to take advantage of DDR, which it supported with a 266 MHz FSB, and the Pentium 4 eventually followed suit. The speed of the module in MHz is one measure of the performance, but the bandwidth of the module that measures how much data it can transfer in one second is more meaningful. The early 266 MHz DDR was also known as PC2100, for its 2100 MB/s bandwidth, 400 MHz DDR is PC3200, and 600 MHz DDR with the PC4800 moniker is just on the horizon. The motherboard must explicitly support DDR for it to be used. Our Athlon 64 system in Chapter 5 uses DDR memory in a dual-channel configuration, which allows the CPU to take advantage of the combined bandwidth of two modules.

Figure 2.6
Crucial DDR2-533 and Corsair DDR-400 DIMMs

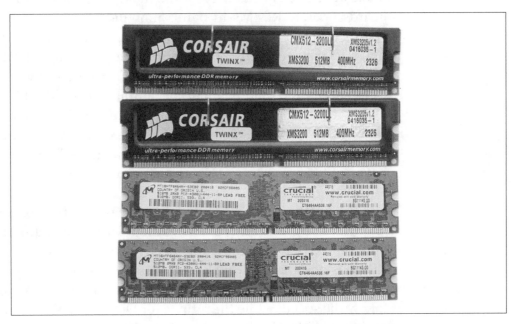

The second generation of Double Data Rate SDRAM is known simply as DDR-2. DDR-2 was introduced at 400 MHz, the same maximum speed as first-generation DDR at the time, but eventually DDR-2 promises to ramp that speed up to 800 MHz, double the initial speed. Keeping with the original module bandwidth rating system of DDR, the 400 MHz DDR-2 is known as PC2-3200, and the 533 MHz module is PC2-4300. DDR-2 operates at 1.8V, compared to 2.5V for the original DDR, which greatly reduces the amount of heat generated. The standard DDR-2 module for desktop use is 240 pins vs. 184 pins for the original DDR, so they aren't physically interchangeable. Intel quickly adopted DDR-2 as the new standard for desktop systems, but AMD didn't rush in, since the greater latency (timing overhead) of DDR-2 cancelled out some of the benefits. Our Intel system in Chapter 4 is built with DDR-2.

The RAM used in the IBM PC came in the form of one bit–wide chips in *Dual Inline Packages,* or *DIP Chips.* As memory chips shrank and capacity grew, they were mounted to small circuit boards called Single Inline Memory Modules (SIMMs), first 8 bits wide (1 byte), and then 32 bits wide (4 bytes). As chips continued to shrink, and capacity and memory buses continued to grow, the

SIMM width was doubled, giving us DIMM. The current DIMM modules are 64 bits wide, and they can be installed in matched pairs on motherboards with dual-channel support, effectively doubling the bandwidth.

RAMBUS, or *RDRAM* technology represents a departure from the step-by-step evolution of RAM we have presented to this point. The original RDRAM Inline Memory Modules (RIMMs) were only 16 bits wide, but they made up in speed what they lacked in module width. Dual-channel mother-boards operate RIMMs in pairs, allowing an effective width of 32 bits at speeds of up to 800 MHz. Not surprisingly, RDRAM modules run awfully hot, and they currently cost about twice as much as DDR modules of the same capacity. As DDR and DDR-2 increased bandwidth through higher clock speeds and dual-channel configurations, RAMBUS attempted to come back with quad-channel (four module) memory banks and even faster clock rates, currently up to 1200 MHz. Despite early chipset support and the announcement by a major manufacturer of a quad-channel motherboard, they have yet to appear as a commercial product.

Original RIMMs must be installed in banks of two for dual-channel operation, and unused banks must be filled with special dummies called Continuity RIMMs (CRIMMS), for electrical signal continuity. The 800 MHz RIMM is designated PC800; 1066 MHz RIMM is PC1066 and the 1200 MHz modules are called PC1200. Note that the module designations for RDRAM follow the speed, while the ratings for DDR and DDR-2 agree with the module bandwidth. There are some signs that the industry is moving to adopt a RIMM nomenclature, as in RIMM800 in place of PC800, before the numbers start conflicting. This will happen when they reach the 1600 MHz module, which would be PC1600—the same as the designation of the original DDR module. Our Intel Pentium 4 in Chapter 6 is built with dual-channel RDRAM.

Figure 2.7
128 MB PC800
RIMM above
CRIMM

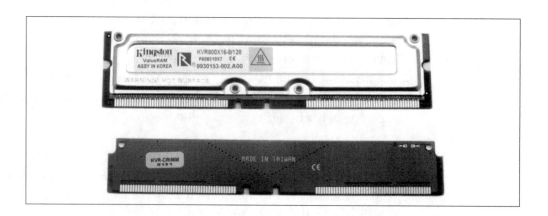

Memory Technology	Designation	Memory Bus Clock Speed[1]	Bus Width	Perfect World Throughput[2]
Double Data Rate (DDR)	PC2-5300[3]	333 MHz	128 bits in dual channel, 64 bits in single channel	10.6 GB/s
	PC2-4300	267 MHz		8.6 GB/s
	PC2-3200	200 MHz		6.4 GB/s
Double Data Rate (DDR)	PC-4800[3]	300 MHz	128 bits in dual channel, 64 bits in single channel	9.6 GB/s
	PC-4300	267 MHz		8.6 GB/s
	PC-3200	200 MHz		6.4 GB/s
RDRAM	PC-1200[3]	600 MHz	32 bits in dual channel with 16-bit modules	4.8 GB/s
	PC-1066	533 MHz		4.3 GB/s
	PC-800	400 MHz		3.2 GB/s
DDR (Original Releases)	PC-2400	150 MHz	Typically 64 bit in older single channel	2.4 GB/s
	PC-2100	133 MHz		2.1 GB/s
	PC-1600	100 MHz		1.6 GB/s

1. *Data is transferred on rising and falling clock, so bus speeds are often reported as double the actual clock speed.*

2. *Throughput for Dual Channel RDRAM, current DDR, or DDR-2 and Single Channel for original DDR.*

3. *Not available at press time.*

Both DDR and RIMM modules are available with the Error Correction Code (ECC) enhancement. ECC memory can correct single-bit errors on the fly and catch multiple-bit errors, unlike the earlier parity error checking, which couldn't correct any errors or identify two-bit flips. ECC memory must be supported by the motherboard, unless it uses ECC onboard technology; and the price premium for ECC memory has almost disappeared with plummeting memory prices.

Video Adapter

There is no good reason to build a new PC with anything less than a 8X Advanced Graphics Port (AGP) adapter or a PCI Express 16X card. In other words, you should always install the latest video card technology your motherboard supports. The original AGP adapters at 1X (single speed) and 2X were 3.3 Volt devices. 4X AGP adapters and the combination 4X/8X are 1.5 Volt devices, while the latest 8X cards support 1.5V or 0.8V. Therefore, some AGP adapters support multiple voltages, but motherboards are designed to work at one voltage or the other. Just make sure you don't buy an AGP adapter that doesn't explicitly support the signaling voltage of your motherboard. PCI Express video adapters have just appeared so they all work in the current PCI Express 16X slot.

As with memory modules, AGP adapters are keyed with a notch in their contact edge so they cannot be installed in an AGP slot that doesn't supply the correct voltage. The early 1X/2X AGP adapters have a notch in the connector edge toward the back of the card (the end with the video connector) and the later 2X/4X cards have a notch toward the front of the connector edge (the front of the case). Universal adapters that support 1.5 or 3.3 Volts at any speed have both notches, as do the new 4X/8X adapters that support 1.5V.

Video Specification	PCI Express	AGP 2.0	AGP 3.0
Internal signaling	Low voltage differential	3.3/1.5 Volt	1.5/0.8 Volt
Peak speeds	16X - 4.0 GB/s	2X = 533 MB/s 4X = 1066 MB/s	4X = 1.0 GB/s[1] 8X = 2.0 GB/s
Slot type	Sized for number of serial channels	Keyed to front or universal (both)	Keyed to front

1. *Rounding down from 1066 MB/s.*

Aside from bus type, the factors affecting video card performance are the graphics processor and the amount of video RAM onboard. The minimum amount of RAM installed on an AGP adapter today is 32 MB, more than enough to display true color at the resolution 17" monitors normally display. However, monitors and standard video adapters are designed to present two-dimensional images (2D). In the world of gaming, the illusion of three-dimensional (3D) space is key to a realistic experience. Video adapters with 3D graphics processors are essentially single-board computers, and they need a lot of memory for texture maps and to support fast panning over an area larger than the display. You can get terrific 3D graphics out of a video adapter with 128 MB of RAM, but the trend is to add more and more, as much as 256 MB, to support 3D graphics processing. One of the penalties of adding RAM to a video card is increased power demand, requiring a bigger power supply and more cooling.

The standard 15-pin high-density connector used for computer monitors since the late 1980s is slowly disappearing from some high-end video adapters. The replacement is the DVI (Digital Video Interface) connector, but aside from plasma displays and recent LCD monitors, most monitors aren't equipped with a DVI connector. A simple port converter, a passive device that takes the legacy analog signals that are still available in the DVI connector and routes them into a standard 15-pin connector, allows you to use any monitor with DVI-only equipped video card. As multimedia PCs increase in popularity, many video adapters are also equipped with an S-Video port so the output can be displayed on a standard television monitor when viewing DVD movies.

Case and Power Supply

Not long ago there was only one power supply standard for ATX PCs, which meant you could concentrate on case geometry (how many drive bays, front panel design) and not worry much about the power supply. Most cases came with a 250-watt ATX supply and for a few bucks more you could upgrade it to 300 watts if you were loading up on higher performance components. However, the rise of power-hungry CPUs, video adapters, and USB-attached peripherals has pushed the entry-level power supply requirement up to 300 watts for most new systems, with 400 watts being a safe bet for the home hobbyist with possible expansion plans. The D925XCV Intel motherboard in our first build is quoted as requiring 200 watts of power in a minimal implementation, and 300 watts when loaded up with memory and heavy USB draws. That doesn't include any adapter cards or drives, so the old 250-watt supply is obviously out of the question.

A few years ago, Intel introduced new Pentium 4 motherboards that require a special 12-volt header (connector) on the power supply in addition to the standard ATX 20-wire connector, which has been adopted for motherboards supporting AMD CPUs as well. Manufacturers implemented the additional power connector in two basic versions: a square four-pin connector, which is installed near the CPU and became the de facto standard, or a six-pin inline connector borrowed from the old AT power supplies that attached near the primary one. The power requirements of some of the latest motherboards have outstripped the original 20-wire ATX connector, so designers have borrowed the 24-wire design used in many servers. Our Chapter 4 build motherboard gives us the option of using a power supply with the 24-wire connector, or using a standard ATX 20-wire connector, supplemented by one of the standard, large-format drive connectors from the power supply. Newer power supplies also feature SATA power connectors for the latest hard drives, but a simple plug-in adapter is available to convert the old connectors to the smaller SATA format. Adapters also exist to convert the 20-wire connector to a 24-wire connector, but that doesn't mean the power supply circuit will produce sufficient current for the motherboard.

Figure 2.8
A standard 20-wire connector and 4-wire 12-volt Pentium 4 connector

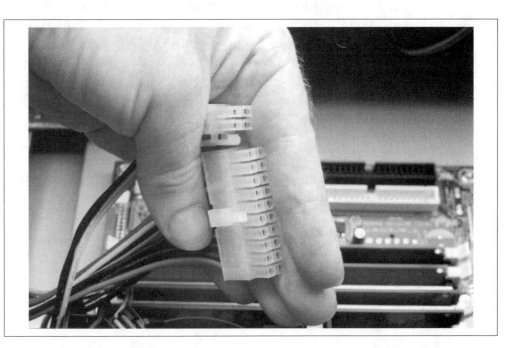

Moving beyond connector compatibility issues, the main figure of merit for a power supply is the power output, in watts. The minimum power supply sold these days is 250 watts, which is enough for basic Socket 478 or Socket A builds. However, new video cards with their own hot processors, cooling fans, and large amounts of video RAM usually list a 300-watt power supply as a minimum requirement, right on the retail box. Many quality cases now come standard with 350- or 400-watt supplies, and options all the way up to 500 watts are available. The problem is that the label ratings on off-brand power supplies may have nothing to do with their capability to actually deliver stable power over time. The best indication of power supply quality is weight, so if your case arrives with a power supply that barely weighs a pound, I'd be skeptical of the rating. The 350W power supply that came with the mail order case for our Athlon 64 build weighed less than a pound, so we replaced it with an off-the-shelf 400W supply from CompUSA. By way of contrast, the stock 350W supply that came with the Antec case we purchased for our Pentium 4 build weighed almost four pounds.

If you're building a high-performance system, take inventory of the parts you plan on building with and run down their power requirements from the documentation or on the Internet, and then size the power supply accordingly. Don't plan on using 100 percent of the rated capacity; it's not all available at the required voltages. Most PC builders figure on loading supplies to a maximum of 70 percent to 80 percent of the capacity. You can derive the power draw of components you purchase from the labels of devices by multiplying the current draw (A) by the voltage (V) for each listed voltage required. Devices like hard drives and DVD recorders require surprisingly little power individually, but it can add up when you start stacking drives. The Memorex DVD recorder in our first build is rated at 0.6A at 12V and 1.1A at 5V, or 12.7 watts, and each 200 GB Seagate Barracuda in the build is listed at .72A at 5V and .35A at 12V, or 7.8W. These numbers aren't necessarily typical; I've seen CD burners rated as much as 25W, and IDE hard drives as high as 15W. If you're building a high-performance system and you don't want to do the math, then spend a little extra for a power supply in the 400W to 500W range.

Cases come in a number of sizes, shapes, and even colors. Sleek, space-age looks are becoming more popular, but be aware that you're paying for a lot of extra plastic that might interfere with ventilation. Horizontal (flat) desktop cases have pretty much disappeared and the mini-ATX designs are not recommended for do-it-yourselfers, due to ventilation problems.

Case Type	Description	Drive Bays	Power Supply	Price
Minitower	Stands upright on desktop (12–18 inches high)	Two or three 5.25-inch bays, two or three 3.5-inch bays	300 watts	$20–$40 (Cases can be too stuffy for hot CPUs.)
Midtower	Stands upright on desktop or on floor (18–24 inches high)	Three or four 5.25-inch bays, three to six 3.5-inch bays	300–400 watts	$25–$100 (Top of the range for Athlon and Pentium 4 power supply.)
Tower	Stands upright on floor (24–36 inches high)	Four or more 5.25-inch bays, three to eight 3.5-inch bays	400–500 watts	$100 on up. (Cases are heavy, but roomy to work in.)

Intelligent Drive Electronics (IDE)

One of the great innovations that appeared about ten years ago was moving the brains of the hard drive from an add-in adapter out onto the hard drive itself. Drive controllers integrated on your motherboard are really just bridges to the system bus. The Basic I/O System (BIOS), which handles all the low-level communications for the PC, works with a fictional picture of the actual hard drive geometry, in terms of the number of heads, platters, and sectors, a sort of idealized pie chart with overlaying concentric rings. The Intelligent Drive Electronics (IDE) on the hard drive translates these parameters, mapping them to the real geometry of the drive. In the case of CD and DVD drives and recorders, the data locations are measured in the time it would take to reach them playing the disc from the start at single speed, but the idea is the same. All the intelligence exists on the drive; hence IDE.

The original IDE interface was defined by the ATA (AT Attachment, as in PC AT) standard, adopted by the American National Standards Institute (ANSI), and amounted to little more than some buffering between the system I/O bus and the intelligent drive. When people refer to an ATA drive, they are referring to an IDE drive; the terms are synonymous. The first improvement to the original IDE standard, the ATA Packet Interface (ATAPI) extended the capability of the interface to work with CDs and other drives.

Serial ATA (SATA) is the latest addition to the IDE family, but these drives, with their new physical interface, are rarely referred to as IDE. Many CDs and DVDs today are still labeled ATAPI devices, but again, this just means they can be attached to an IDE controller. Performance enhancements included Extended IDE (EIDE) and Fast ATA; these were rolled into the basic IDE standard. The slower transfer modes use Polled I/O (PIO), whereas the faster modes use Direct Memory Access (DMA), reading the data directly from the cache memory on the drive into system memory. IDE drives using the two fastest Ultra DMA (UDMA) modes must be attached with a special 80-conductor parallel ribbon cable. This cable has the same number of connectors as the standard 40-conductor parallel ribbon cable, but includes a ground every other wire for noise shielding. SATA drives have dispensed with ribbon cables altogether, replacing them with a faster serial interface.

Transfer Type	Transfer Rate
PIO Mode 4	16.6 MB/s
DMA Mode 1	13.3 MB/s
DMA Mode 2	16.6 MB/s
Ultra DMA/33	33 MB/s
Ultra DMA/66	66 MB/s
UDMA/100 or ATA100	100 MB/s
ATA133	133 MB/s
SATA 150[1]	150 MB/s

1. *SATA 300 (300 MB/s) and SATA 600 (600 MB/s) planned.*

Figure 2.9
Western Digital
SecureConnect
SATA cable

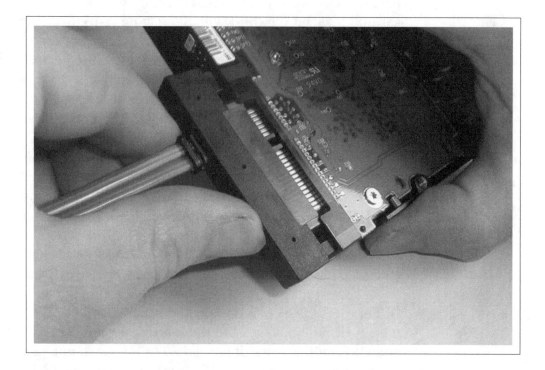

Until recently, RAID systems were very expensive and pretty much limited to network servers and other enterprise hardware. There are a dozen different levels of RAID implementation, but only three are supported by IDE controllers and practical for do-it-yourselfers. RAID arrays can offer two distinct advantages over an individual IDE drive: performance and reliability. The first

RAID implementation, known as *RAID 0*, spreads your data over two or four IDE drives, which appear as single logical drive to the PC. This improves performance through striping reads and writes because the drives are appreciably slower than the controllers. Unfortunately, this increase comes at a loss of reliability, since if one drive fails, all your data is lost.

The second RAID implementation is known as *RAID 1*, and it writes all data to two drives, or two sets of drives, simultaneously. This creates a mirror image of all your data, so if one drive or set of drives fails, nothing is lost. RAID 1 offers a performance increase on reads but not on writes. RAID 10 (0+1) combines RAID 0 and RAID 1, giving you increased performance and reliability.

Small Computer Systems Interface (SCSI)

The Small Computer Systems Interface (SCSI) is older than the IDE interface, and is still champion when it comes to connecting high-performance drives to servers and workstations. SCSI controllers take the opposite approach of the simple and inexpensive IDE controllers, by adding a whole new bus to the PC. With the exception of the cheapest SCSI (pronounced "scuzzy") adapters that occasional shipped with scanners or other peripherals, original SCSI adapters could support up to 7 devices; later this was increased to 15. This includes any combination of devices, hard drives, CD and DVD drives and recorders, proprietary optical drives, tape drives, scanners, and other peripherals both inside and outside the PC.

There are two types of internal cables in use with SCSI devices: the older 50-wire ribbon cable and the 68-wire Low Voltage Differential (LVD) ribbon cable. The LVD cable arranges all the wires in twisted pairs over which the differential (mirror image) signals are passed between the drives and controller.

Level	Known As	Number of Devices	Maximum Transfer Speed	Bus Width
SCSI-1	SCSI	7 (8 w/ controller)	5 MB/s	8 bits
SCSI-2	Fast SCSI	7	10 MB/s	8 bits
	Fast Wide SCSI	15 (16 w/ controller)	20 MB/s	16 bits
SCSI-3	Ultra SCSI	7	20 MB/s	8 bits
	Ultra-wide SCSI	15	40 MB/s	16 bits
	Ultra 2 SCSI	7	40 MB/s	8 bits
	Ultra 2 Wide SCSI or Ultra 80	15	80 MB/s	16 bits
	Ultra 3 SCSI	7	80 MB/s	8 bits
	Ultra 3 Wide SCSI or Ultra 160	15	160 MB/s	16 bits
SCSI 4	Ultra 4 SCSI	15	320 MB/s	16 bits (support for 8-bit bus dropped)

Figure 2.10
LVD cable with terminator and 50-wire original SCSI cable

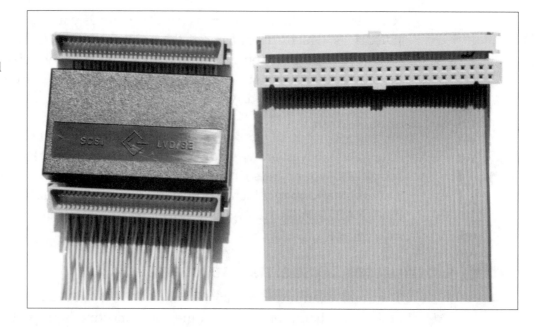

The SCSI bus is inherently more reliable than the IDE interface, due in part to the large number of grounds in the ribbon cables to provide protection against electrical noise and cross-talk, and in part due to termination. In order to eliminate signals reflecting back from devices at the ends of the bus, SCSI buses have always required termination; installation of a dummy load to absorb any leftover power at the ends of the bus. External devices are either equipped with a switch to enable termination or a dummy load is attached to the open SCSI port of the last device on the chain.

Internal SCSI devices were traditionally equipped with either a jumper or a series of resistor packs that were removed when the device was not at the end of the bus (the last device on the ribbon cable). Starting with Ultra 2 SCSI devices, the termination was moved onto the ribbon cable, and the devices shipped with the termination disabled. Early SCSI controllers were also equipped with a jumper or switch to enable termination when they were on one end of the bus, and to disable termination if both internal and external devices were attached. Newer SCSI controllers give you the option to enable or disable termination in software.

Comparing Drive Performance

With the exception of floppy drives, which are all essentially the same, drive pricing is driven by capacity and performance. Capacity figures are easy enough to compare for hard drives and tape drives (CDs and DVDs are fixed capacity). The drive that holds the most gigabytes (GBs) wins. Whether or not you need all that storage and how much extra you are willing to pay for it is up to you, but for most people the performance is more important than the capacity, which is excessive to begin with.

Drive seek time is an average measure of how long it takes the drive to position the read/write head over a random location on the drive to begin reading or writing a file. This speed is measured in milliseconds (ms, thousandths of a second) and is usually less than 10 ms for hard drives. A similar measure exists for CD and DVD drives, but the seek times are five to ten times slower. Whereas the seek time was once considered the figure of merit when shopping for drives, it has been supplanted by the transfer rate for both hard drives and CD/DVDs, and the spindle speed for hard drives.

The transfer rate for hard drives is measured in MB/s, and just about all new ATA hard drives are rated as SATA 150 or ATA 133. It means that the ATA controller can use DMA to read or write the cache memory buffer on the hard drive at 150 or 133 MB/s. Given the relatively small size of the buffer, usually between 1–8 MB, and the relatively large size of many files, this isn't a terribly useful measure of hard drive performance. Somewhat more useful is the drive-to-buffer or buffer-to drive rating, which falls short of the cache to controller speed for both ATA and SCSI drives.

Both the transfer measurements and the seek time are related to the spindle speed of the drive. The *spindle speed* is simply a measure of how fast the platters are spinning inside the drive. This is important because the faster they are spinning, the quicker any point on the drive comes under the read/write head and the faster the data can be streamed into the buffer of cache memory on the drive. For this reason, drives with higher spindle speeds, measured in Revolutions Per Minute (RPM), also tend to have larger caches. The slowest IDE drives on the market today have a spindle speed of 4,500 RPM and the fastest run at 10,000 RPM. SCSI drives start off around 7,200 RPM and run as fast as 15,000 RPM.

CD and DVD drives are first and foremost rated by their *multiplier speed,* which describes how many times faster they are turning than the equivalent home entertainment system playing a music CD or a movie. Single speed (1X) for CDs is defined as 150 KB/s and single speed for DVDs is 1,385 KB/s. Looking at the numbers for faster devices, a 50X CD reads data at 7.5 MB/s (7,500 KB/s) and a 16X DVD at 22.16 MB/s (22,160 KB/s). CD and DVD drives are much slower than hard drives, and derive little benefit from being attached to fast interfaces.

Both CD Recorders (CDRs) and DVD Recorders have three speeds associated with them, which are expressed, for example, as 16/10/40. The first number is the maximum write speed, the second is the maximum rewrite speed, and the third is the maximum read speed. A fast write speed for CDRs is 32X, and 12X is a fast DVD recorder. A 32X CDR can record, or *burn*, an average length music CD (50 minutes) in about three minutes, including session information. Rewrite speeds are usually lower (and never greater) than write speeds, and in all cases the media you purchase must be rated at least as fast as the drive. The maximum read speed for recorders is usually a little slower than the maximum read speed for plain CD or DVD drives.

One commonly overlooked factor in purchasing a recorder is the recording software. Do not buy a CDR without software unless you already own CDR software purchased as a shrink-wrapped retail package. OEM software purchased with one CDR will not work with another brand. Media cost is always a consideration in buying a drive, particularly with the latest DVDR technologies, such as dual layer.

Drive Type	Capacity	Interface	Brand Names	Performance	Price Range
Hard drive	40–300 GB	IDE (SATA150 or ATA 133)	Maxtor, Western Digital, Seagate	4,500–10,000 RPM, 1–8 MB cache	$40–$300, based on capacity and spindle RPM
Hard drive	18–180 GB	SCSI	Maxtor, Seagate	7,200–15,000 RPM, 4–16 MB cache	$75–$800, based on capacity and spindle RPM
CD drive	680 MB	IDE or SCSI	Mitsumi, Acer, Toshiba	50X or higher	$10–$30, more for SCSI
CDR drive	680 MB	IDE, SCSI, USB (External)	NEC, Toshiba, Matsushita, Ricoh, HP	32/58/32, write/ rewrite/read	$25–$50, most for external SCSI
DVD drive	18 GB max (must eject to flip)	IDE, SCSI	Toshiba, Sony, Pioneer, Hitachi	56X reading CD, 16X reading DVD	$20–$50, more for SCSI
DVD-R and DVD RAM drives	4.7 GB / 9.4 GB (dual layer)	IDE, SCSI, USB (external)	Pioneer, Panasonic, NEC, Toshiba	12X DVD-R, 12X DVD+R, 8X DVD RAM	$40–$120, depending on speed, interface
Tape drives, Travan or DAT	Travan 4–20 GB, DAT 4–240 GB	IDE, SCSI (oldest Travans used floppy)	Seagate, Exabyte, HP	Travan is slow, DAT 30 MB/minute– 300 MB/minute	$150–$450 for Travan, $400– $5000 for DAT
Cartridge drives (falling out of use)	Zip 100 MB or 250 MB, Jaz 2 GB	IDE, USB, SCSI	Iomega, NEC, Panasonic	Zip speed comparable to CD, Jaz to hard drive	$10–$50, 100 MB or 250 MB Zip, $250 for Jaz
Floppy drive	1.44 MB, 120 MB Super Floppy (LS-120)	Floppy	LS-120, NEC, Imation, Mitsubishi	Slow	Floppy drive $10, LS-120 $50–$100

Modems

More than half of Americans with Internet connections still use a dial-up modem. The original telephone modems worked by modulating an audio carrier frequency that could be transmitted through plain old telephone lines with a signal that could be decoded into binary data, 1's and 0's. To transmit and receive information, the device had to perform MOdulation and DE-Modulation, giving rise to the name MODEM. Early PC modems worked at 300 b/s and steadily improved, passing the fax speed of 9,600 b/s right up to 33 Kb/s (33,000 bits/second). There the technology hit the wall, and a new solution was needed.

The breakthrough was to dispense with the digital-to-analog conversion on the downstream side (from the Internet Service provider [ISP] to your home) and transmit digital data. This technique can boost speed to 56 Kb/s, although you'll never see more than 53 Kb/s in the United States because of FCC regulations. Differences between competing standards were resolved several years ago, leaving us with the standard V.92 56 Kb/s modem.

Even with the great advances in dial-up modem speed over the years, there remain a few problems with access and speed. Most people who have 56 Kb/s modems won't see speeds much over 40 Kb/s on a sustained basis, unless their telephone infrastructure is in pretty good shape. Overloaded telephone infrastructure and ISP modem pools lead to frequent disconnects and busy signals. If you spend a lot of time online, you'll quickly tire of waiting for big chunks of information to download to your computer. Another problem is that the modem ties up your phone line, so unless you have an extra phone line you can't make or receive calls while online.

There are two mainstream alternatives to dial-up telephone modems: cable modems and Digital Subscriber Line (DSL) modems. Cable modems claim transfer rates as high as 43 Mb/s, and Asynchronous DSL (ASDL) modems as high as 8 Mb/s. Well, forget about ever seeing speeds that high. Real-world cable modem speeds run from the hundreds of kilobits per second to around 2 Mb/s, and consumer DSL packages steer clear of promising download speeds over 1.5 Mb/s, which costs extra.

The first consideration when it comes to choosing between cable and DSL is which (if either) is available to you. Not all cable companies offer cable modem access, and not all people live close enough to a telephone central office to get DSL. Another consideration, if both services are available to you, is package deals. Some cable Internet providers cut you a nice discount, providing you are already connected for cable TV; and some online services like AOL have DSL arrangements with local telephone companies. In either case, if you are paying for an extra phone line for your PC, you can get rid of it, and the Internet connection will always be open, 24 hours a day.

Both cable and consumer DSL are slower at uploading data from your PC to the Internet than downloading, but this isn't particularly important for most users. Two more modem technologies are Integrated Services Digital Network (ISDN) and satellite, but ISDN is being rapidly replaced by DSL and, until I meet somebody with a satellite Internet connection, I'll pass on commenting. When comparing prices, remember that cable and DSL services both replace your dial-up ISP, so if you were paying $21.95/month for dial-up, you can apply that money to the new bill. Don't run out and buy a cable or DSL modem before ordering the service! They might require you to purchase the modem through a particular retail chain, or offer one for next to nothing as a signing bonus.

Modem Type	Requirements	PC Connection	Speed[1]	Costs
56 Kb/s modem	None, although if your ISP isn't in your area code, it gets expensive	Internal PCI modem or external serial port modem	53 Kb/s max in U.S. (by law), lower connection speeds normal	$5–$20 fax/voice modem
Cable modem	Local cable carrier must offer service	External using 10/100BaseT network adapter or USB	1–2 Mb/s download, 128–384 Kb/s upload	$30–$75, but don't buy before ordering service
DSL (Digital Subscriber Line)	Local telco must offer service, distance limitations	External using network connection or USB. Earlier, an internal PCI adapter was common.	1.5 Mb/s or 768 Kb/s download, 384 Kb/s upload	Usually sold by the telco with the package for a nominal price

1. *56 Kb/s modem speed depends greatly on local conditions. Cable modem speeds depend on how many people in your neighborhood are using the service, as the bandwidth is shared. DSL packages are priced at different points according to connection speed.*

Sound Cards

Most people want sound capability in home PCs, but only serious game players, musicians, and people attempting to replace their stereos need to look past the most basic adapter. Most motherboards include basic sound capabilities at no extra cost, and an extremely capable PCI card with 5.1 Surround Sound can be purchased for $10. However, there is a high-end market that is focused as much on speakers as sound cards. You can spend $100 or more on a sound card if you want, and the best way to see the latest, greatest offering is to pick up a PC magazine. However, the integrated sound capabilities on most brand name motherboards are increasingly more than adequate for even dedicated gamers and audiophiles. Both the Intel motherboard in our Chapter 4 build and the ASUS motherboard in our Chapter 5 build incorperate eight-channel (7.1 sound) onboard.

Network Adapters

As with sound capability, many motherboards now integrate 10/100BaseT or even Gigabit network support. I am entirely brand blind when it comes to add-in network adapters. The cheapest $5 adapter is fine by me. Network cards are the single exception to my "don't buy what you don't need now" rule, because the adapter that costs $5 from your mail order parts vendor may cost $40 in a retail box. If you are purchasing a network adapter to connect to a cable modem, the story ends here, but if you are considering a home Local Area Network (LAN) to share resources, including Internet access, I would seriously consider going wireless. When you take into account the cost of network cables, adapters, and a hub, you won't need to add much on top to go to a wireless LAN. Just don't confuse wireless home networking products (Ethernet) with wireless phone modems (cell phone accessories) when shopping online.

Video Monitors

Monitors have slowly gotten cheaper, so that 15" monitors are often sold for less than $100 and brand-name, flat-screen 17" monitors are available for under $150. A 15" LCD monitor is currently around $225, and large plasma screens used for presentation cost several thousand. We went over the factors differentiating monitor quality in Chapter 1. LCD screens have an additional figure of merit, the viewing angle, the wider the better.

Technology	Sizes in Use	Features (best/worst)	Quality Measure (best/average)	Price/Size (smallest/largest)
Plasma	42"/50"	Best viewing distance, lowest resolution	Contrast Ratio 750:1/600:1	$2500/$5500
LCD	15"/32"	Space saving, low power, mediocre resolution	Contrast Ratio 500:1/300:1	$225/$1725
CRT	17"/21"	High resolution, heavy and bulky	Dot pitch .22/.28	$100/$350

There is a pretty good correlation between brand name and quality for monitors, so be careful when buying an OEM or a no-name brand. Often the hardware is identical to a name brand, but the final labor-intensive steps in quality control and focusing are skipped. You have two choices when it comes to buying a monitor: you can either walk into your local retailer and buy one off the shelf, hopefully on sale or with a rebate, or you can mail order one. Image quality is a subjective measure as some people value brightness over sharpness or perceive colors differently, so purchasing through a retail outlet with active monitors on display will let you determine what's right for you. As always, another problem with mail order is shipping cost, which can run more than $30 for monitors. If there is a problem and you need to return it, your savings will evaporate in a hurry.

Figure 2.11
Nvidia PCI Express
adapter supports
dual DVI monitors

Printers and Scanners

Almost everyone will want to own a printer with his or her PC, and scanners are increasingly common purchases as their prices have fallen to less than $50. In short, a variety of color inkjet printers are available between $50–$200. Frequent replacement of the inkjet cartridges is a big hidden expense. When shopping for an inkjet, go to a retail store that will let you print some test pages and check the price of the replacement cartridges, because you'll be buying a lot of them.

If you do a serious amount of printing (more than pages a day), buy a laser printer. Excellent quality B&W laser printers sell in the $200–$300 range. The more expensive lasers are intended for the really high-volume office environment, and offer few advantages for moderate volume users. Entry-level color laser printers have fallen into the $400–$500 range, but they weight more than the average person can comfortably carry around the house and they are slower than less-expensive B&W lasers. Unless you print a lot of color, I would suggest a B&W laser for text and an inexpensive color inkjet for color.

A good USB scanner can be had for as little as $30 with a rebate. All flat-bed scanners do a pretty good job on color pictures, although professional graphics artists and photographers will require something a little more up-scale. If you are scanning pictures for the Internet or to e-mail to friends, use the lowest resolution available and save the image using Joint Photography Experts Group (JPEG) compression. Also, if you are buying a scanner specifically to do Optical Character Recognition (OCR), which is conversion of existing print documents into word processor files, make sure that the OCR software that comes with your scanner is a full version and not a 30-day trial.

Chapter 3

Before You Assemble Your PC

The following checklist should be completed when you order PC parts to make sure you have enough components to assemble a working PC:

❏ **ATX case and power supply**   Note that both the Pentium 4 and Athlon 64 motherboards have special power supply requirements (see Chapter 2).

❏ **ATX motherboard and CPU**   Socket 775 or 478 for Pentium 4, depending on CPU model. Socket 939 or 754 for Athlon 64, depending on the CPU model, and Socket 939 or 940 for Athlon 64 FX, depending on the CPU model. Socket A for Athlon or Duron, Socket 478 for Celeron.

❏ **RAM**   DDR-2 for systems supporting it (Pentium 4 in Socket 775 at press time), two matched modules for dual-channel operation. DDR for motherboards supporting it, two matched modules for dual-channel operation. RIMM for motherboards supporting it (Intel CPUs only), continuity modules required if all sockets not populated.

❏ **Video**   4X/8X AGP adapter for 1.5V AGP-capable motherboards, PCI Express 16X for motherboards supporting PC Express. If the motherboard has an integrated video adapter, none is required.

❏ **Hard drive**   40GB IDE drive or larger, SATA if supported by the motherboard, otherwise ATA 100 or ATA 133 compatible with 80-conductor cable.

❑ **CD/DVD**   CD-ROM or CD recorder, DVD-ROM or DVD recorder. Any of these can be used to install the operating system and software drivers from CD.

❑ **Keyboard**   Keyboard with PS/2 style connector.

❑ **Mouse**   Mouse with PS/2 style connector.

❑ **Monitor**   15" or larger monitor. DVI-capable monitor or adapter for video adapters with DVI only ports.

❑ **Operating system**   Windows or Linux on CD, any version. Note that some new components, particularly peripherals, require recent operating system release.

The following are optional but often useful, and some may come integrated on the motherboard.

❑ **Modem**   56-Kb/s V.92 modem.

❑ **Sound card**   PCI sound card if the motherboard doesn't have integrated sound or the integrated capabilities fall short of your needs.

❑ **Floppy drive**   1.44 MB 3.5" floppy drive. Note that a floppy drive will actually be required if the operating system CD doesn't contain a compatible driver for the hard drive controller when you install the operating system for the first time.

❑ **Network adapter**   10/100BaseT network adapter or Gigabit adapter, if not integrated in the motherboard. Adapter choice depends on the requirements of your network environment.

❑ **Speakers**   Speakers with separate power cord and adapter. Subwoofer required for Surround Sound, along with as many as seven additional speakers in an eight-channel configuration.

❑ **Switched power strip**   With surge protector.

Handling Parts and General Assembly Guidelines

Walking across a carpet can generate a static electric charge of 30,000 volts or more on your body. This is often manifested as a spark leaping from your hand to a doorknob or another person, creating a shock you both can feel. That same discharge, harmless to people (and doorknobs) because of the minute amount of electrical current involved, can ruin expensive computer components in a flash. Other activities that can generate static electricity include removing Styrofoam-encased parts from shipping boxes, taking off a jacket or sweater, or even sitting on a chair and gesturing during a conversation. That's the bad news.

The good news is that you can avoid building up a static electric charge, or at least zapping your components, by taking a few precautions. Most important, don't unpack your parts or assemble your PC in a room where you routinely receive static electric shocks. Next, get in the habit of frequently touching an electrical ground as you work. This ground can be a screw on the faceplate of an electrical outlet, a cold water pipe, or the metal casing of any electrical appliance or tool that uses a three-prong plug. If you plan to do a lot of PC work, it pays to pick up a $10 outlet tester at the local home improvement center to see if the grounds on your outlets are wired properly.

Make sure you keep your components in their static-proof shipping bags when you aren't handling them, and never pick up a component after crossing a room or wrestling with some packaging without grounding yourself first. If you have a damp basement in your home, this is the ideal place to assemble a PC, because humidity reduces static electric discharges.

If the neighborhood children flock to your house to chase each other around, sparks flying, you may consider the extra precautions of a grounding strap. Any decent electronics store will sell you a Velcro wristband with an inline 1 Megaohm resistor and an alligator clip that can be attached to the nearest ground. These are often recommended (or required) in the documentation that comes with your computer parts. The only drawbacks with grounding straps are that they are designed for sitting and working in one place, and they tend to breed overconfidence, making people forget the simple precautions against static discharge. There is also a danger of entanglement when working in an area cluttered with objects such as camera tripods and lights, which is why you won't see one in any of our assembly pictures.

Figure 3.1
Inexpensive grounding strap

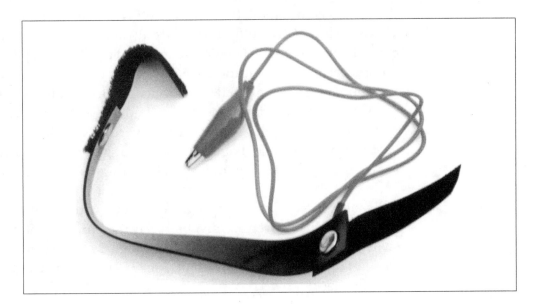

The other primary danger to your computer components, other than dropping them on the floor, is the electricity generated by your computer power supply. Computers are often powered up with the cover off when first assembled, just to make sure they work and that the front panel LED leads aren't connected to the motherboard backward. Even in the old days, before ATX power supplies, this was probably a bigger source of component damage than static electricity, as technicians and hobbyists alike would forget that the power supply was turned on and proceed to add or remove an adapter. This can cause power spikes and short circuits, which can easily damage adapters and motherboards.

Screws fumbled into the case while trying to secure an adapter in a "hot" system are another danger. Another dangerous scenario is when you drop a screw into the guts of the case during an assembly procedure and you use another screw to finish the job, intending to hunt down the escapee later. Never wait for later to retrieve a lost screw because it is just too easy to forget about it until it shows up jammed in just the wrong place under the motherboard, shorting out the whole system. Also, as a final check before powering up any newly built system, pick the whole case up and tilt it in every direction, listening for the telltale sound of a rolling screw. If you hear one, even if you can't get the sound to repeat, stop in your tracks and find it, even if it requires some disassembly.

ATX power supplies and motherboards, although generally easier to work with than the older AT design they replaced, create one new problem. With the old power supplies, if the switch was off and the fan was silent, it was safe to work on the system and you could use the case as a ground. The new ATX power supplies are equipped with an override switch on the back of the supply to turn the power supply off, because the supply remains partially on even when the PC is turned off with the front panel power switch. This is because ATX motherboards are always receiving a trickle of current to control the power switch logic and to afford the PC the capability to wake up on a preset alarm. In addition, to support the capability of network adapters and modems to wake the PC if activity occurs, a 720mA current is always available on the 5V supply to the PCI adapters. Not many people will remember to turn off that power supply override switch on the back of the PC every time they should. For this reason, I suggest plugging in the PC through a switched power strip with a switch that lights when it's on.

Finally, most power supplies are equipped with a recessed 115V/230V on the back of the power supply, between the cord socket and the override switch. The voltage that shows is the voltage that is selected. Power supplies sold in the United States are usually set to 115V in the factory, but it pays to double-check.

Figure 3.2
Voltage selector
switch

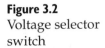

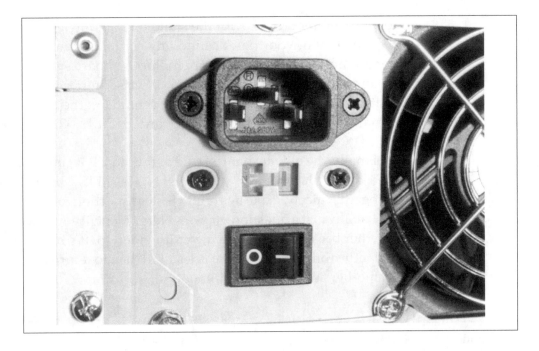

Figure 3.2
Voltage selector
switch

The only tool you absolutely need for assembling most PCs is a Phillips screwdriver. Nutdrivers come in handy for inserting brass standoffs to support the motherboard, but you can use a socket, adjustable wrench, or even pliers, as long as you're careful not to create brass chips. Some manufacturers recommend using a nutdriver or a screwdriver for levering down the heatsink clip, but I strongly advise doing it with your thumb if you can. If the tool should slip off the heatsink clip and smash into the motherboard, I doubt the warranty people will have a sense of humor about it. A large workspace isn't necessary, but a proven grounding point and good lighting are crucial, and a flashlight often comes in handy.

Before you begin to assemble your PC, look through all the pictures in this book (even the ones for the CPU types you aren't building) to become familiar with the steps involved. Your exact build might combine features from the three different builds here, and as chipset manufacturers provide new functionality for the motherboard makers, new combinations of memory types for the different CPUs are expected. Although each of our three systems tells a complete illustrated assembly story, we vary the order of the procedures and highlight certain features with each build. For example, our lead Pentium 4 system is built with an SATA RAID, PCI Express video, and DDR-2 RAM. Our Athlon 64 features dual-channel DDR, and a reinforced SATA cable, while our older Pentium 4 system is built with RDRAM and with both SCSI and IDE disk subsystems.

Read through the documentation that comes with all the parts you purchase. While much of the material is boilerplate, different manufacturers like to play different tricks with the standards, and in all cases, the instructions that come with your parts trump any conflicting instructions in this book. For example, there is no standard for motherboard settings; the motherboard documentation must be consulted. It's also important to confirm that any switch or jumper setting shown as "default" in the motherboard manual is actually selected on your motherboard, because often it isn't.

Finally, the old mechanics' rule of thumb, "If it jams, force it—If it breaks, it needed replacing anyway," DOES NOT APPLY HERE. If your parts don't fit together nicely, make a careful visual inspection to find out why. Although it's usually just a question of proper alignment, it could well be they don't fit together because they were never intended to. It's better to feel a little silly and return one good part that doesn't fit than to return two parts that don't fit each other and are ruined to boot!

	Chapter 4	Chapter 5	Chapter 6
Case and power supply	Midtower—350W	Midtower—400W	Tower—300W w/ 12V for P4
CPU and socket	Pentium 4 560 at 3.6 GHz, Socket 775 LGA	AMD Athlon 64 3800+ in Socket 939	2.0 GHz Intel Pentium 4, Socket 478
Motherboard features	PCI Express adapter support, integrated 7.1 sound, SATA support with RAID 0/1	AGP 8X support, 5.1 sound, integrated RAID support for SATA and IDE	Sound, 10/100BaseT network, USB ports and hub, ATA 100, AGP 4X support
RAM installed	1 GB DDR2-533 (PC2-4300), Dual Channel	1 GB DDR-400 (PC-3200), Dual Channel	256 MB RIMM (PC-800), Dual Channel
Highlights	Screwless 5.25" drive mounts, 120mm exhaust fan, CPU heatsink fan hood	Wireless networking adapter, dual-layer DVD recorder, stress-relief SATA cable	Adaptec 160 MB/s SCSI and IDE RAID, USB 2.0 adapter

Problems to Watch Out For

Six basic things can go wrong before or during PC assembly that will prevent it from powering up and operating properly:

❏ **Faulty connections**   This is the most common problem, and it includes the following: improperly made data cable connections to the drives or motherboard; switch, fan, and LED connections partially made or connected to the wrong points on the motherboard; partially inserted power connectors; poorly seated CPUs and memory modules; improperly installed heatsinks; and Adapter cards not fully seated in the bus connectors. Illustrations follow this discussion.

❑ **Improper settings** These can be jumpers or switches on the motherboard, the voltage switch on the power supply, or software settings made in CMOS Setup after the initial power-up. The wrong voltage selection on the power supply (115V or 230V) will ruin components. Improper settings in CMOS Setup will generally result in resource conflicts, poor performance, or inconsistent behavior and lockups. In all instances, the only source for motherboard settings is the small manual that ships with the motherboard or the settings printed on the motherboard itself. Most new motherboards can automatically select all of the proper manufacturer-recommended settings for the CPU and are sold with this option selected as the default, but always double-check the actual settings against the manual.

❑ **DOA (Dead On Arrival) parts** Although this problem is less common than generally thought, especially given the poor packaging used by many mail order vendors and incredibly low-component pricing, you might encounter a DOA component. Troubleshooting which component is dead often requires access to a working PC to swap out parts (see Chapter 8). This is the best reason to buy your motherboard, CPU, RAM, case, and video adapter (the minimum needed to get a live screen) from the same vendor to simplify return issues.

❑ **Incompatible or poorly selected components** This is rare with the motivated do-it-yourselfer, but a careless selection of parts from an Internet site may leave you with a Pentium 4 LGA CPU for a Socket 478 motherboard or an 8X AGP adapter for a motherboard supporting PCI Express. The best way to avoid this type of problem is to keep a written list of selected parts and their requirements as you shop, and not make snap decisions on attractively priced components.

❑ **Carelessness** Dropping parts, leaving loose screws rattling around the case, wearing a wool sweater and pulling it off over your long hair, and then picking up the CPU without grounding yourself . . . all these things happen. The only antidote for carelessness is staying alert, but not by drinking a coffee over your open PC!

❑ **Ventilation** Whether suggested or required by the various component manufacturers, a high-performance system should be built with at least one additional exhaust fan on the back of the case and a front intake fan. Even more important, don't operate your PC in an enclosed space, like a compartment in a custom-built computer desk, where the airflow around the front, back, or side vents is restricted. Some case designs feature a side grille with a fan hood positioned over the CPU heatsink fan, giving it a direct path to the outside air. This leads us to a final point, which is you can't operate a high-performance PC in a hot environment without running into problems. A room temperature of 100°F or 38°C guarantees that the temperature inside the case is at least as high, violating the operating conditions for multiple component manufacturers.

Faulty Connections

The most common mistake of new PC builders is not making sure adapter cards are properly seated in the slots before closing up the case. Even if the adapter seats properly when you initially push it into the slot, it may pop partially out again when another adapter is seated in an adjacent slot. Paradoxically, the leading reason for PCI and AGP adapters to pop out of their slots is the insertion of the screw that is intended to hold them in place. This happens because the PCI slots, and even more the AGP slot, are located further from the back of the case than the original ISA slots were. When the screw forces down the port end of the adapter, it might pivot on the back edge of the slot, causing the front edge of the adapter to lever partially out of position. Some of the newer video adapters and slots are designed with a retention mechanism to prevent just this failure. The ASUS motherboard in our Chapter 5 build has an AGP locking mechanism.

Figure 3.3
PCI adapter partially out of the slot

A similar result often occurs when memory modules are inserted unevenly. This is why we emphasize seating a module with two thumbs and letting the white locking levers at the ends of the memory slots raise into place on their own as the module is properly seated. Wedging the module in on one end first and pulling up on the locking levers to encourage it into place can damage the memory slot or result in a failed insertion, particularly with DDR-2 modules in stiff sockets.

Figure 3.4
Partially seated
DIMM

The most likely reason for a system to fail to power up once it's plugged in and the switch is pressed on the front panel is that the power switch lead is attached to the motherboard improperly. This can result from a mistake in reading the motherboard manual or on-board markings, but it can also occur simply because the connection block for panel leads is dense with tightly spaced posts. Squinting through a maze of wires in a poorly lit work area can lead to all sorts of missed connections. The power switch, a two-lead connector, is shown in the following with only one half of the connector on a post.

Figure 3.5
Power switch
missing the post

All of the new CPUs are keyed so they can only be inserted in the proper orientation, but partial insertion is still a possibility with all except the latest Pentium 4 LGA processors. This is more common with the older CPU types such as the Slot A Athlon and the Slot 1 Pentium III, because the edge connectors rely on spring force to make good contact with the processor cartridges, and therefore require strong pressure to insert and seat fully. Normally, when a slot-type system is powered up with a partially seated CPU, the power LED comes on, the drives whir, but the screen remains dead. Socket CPUs can also be partially inserted, usually due to being pushed into place with the locking lever not completely open or through sheer carelessness. The lever can be closed with the CPU cocked at an angle and, in some cases, the heat sink can even be locked in place over it. If you force a heatsink down over a partially seated CPU you can damage the package.

Figure 3.6
Failed CPU
insertion

The most problematic drive connection is always the floppy drive. The connectors on the drives are only rarely boxed and keyed, and sometimes labeling for the pin1 end of the connector is hard to find. The ribbon cables can be put on backwards, forced on, missing a full row of the two rows of pins, or even missing one set of pins at one of the ends of the connector. Some floppy cabling problems are immediately apparent, because the small LED on the front of the drive stays permanently lit once the system is powered up.

If you encounter floppy drive problems, undo and remake the connection, even if you have to remove the drive again to get a good look at it. The hardest cabling problem to spot is when to two pins on the down end miss the connector and are simply bent out of the way. When the cable is removed, the pins will still appear straight if you sight down the rows, and the connector will continue to mate improperly until you notice the bent pins and bend them back.

Figure 3.7
Floppy ribbon cable connector missing two pins on end

Ribbon cables also are prone to failure when poorly constructed or removed and remade a number of times. This is due to the lack of a large plastic header on the cable, which forces you to pull on the ribbon cable itself if you want to undo the connection, though quality cables will include a pull tab. If the snaps fail on a connector header and it begins to fall apart, don't even think about pressing it back together, just get a new one.

Figure 3.8
Ribbon cable connector failure

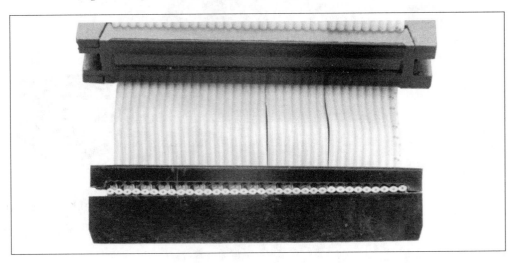

One last problem that deserves mention, although it is not a traditional connector issue, is using the wrong screws in the wrong places. This simple mechanical issue can lead to stripped threads, dangerous metal flakes, and endless frustration. There are three types of screws used in most computers, not including variations in head design. Fine-thread screws are used for floppy drives, CD/DVD drives, and in some instances for motherboard installation. The thinner of the coarse-thread screws are used for hard drives, mounting most motherboards, adapter hold-downs, and case cover screws. The fatter coarse-thread screws are not found in many PCs, but when they are, they are used exclusively for case cover screws.

Figure 3.9
The three types
of screws

Standard Connections Outside the Case

The time to double-check that the voltage switch on the back of your power supply is set correctly for your power grid is before you insert the power cord. The proper voltage for your country, 115V for the United States, should be showing on the switch. The power cord can't be inserted improperly, but it can be inserted too shallowly, so make sure it pushes in a good ½ inch. The override rocker switch, if so equipped, should be switched on by pushing in the side labeled 1.

Figure 3.10
Connecting the
power cord

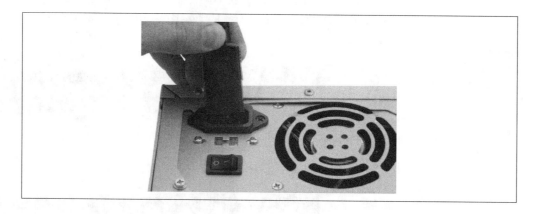

The keyboard and mouse ports are right next to each other and both use PS/2 style connectors. Almost all ports and connectors are color coded, purple for the keyboard and green for the mouse, to help you keep from interchanging them. If you get them backward, it won't hurt anything, but you'll probably get a "keyboard not present" error on boot.

Figure 3.11
Connecting the keyboard and mouse

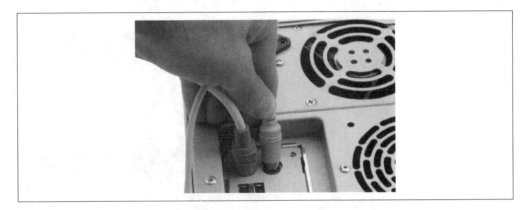

The analog monitor connector is a high-density, 15-pin D-shell arranged in three rows, although a few pins are normally left out. Be careful that you get the orientation correct (it will only go on one way) and that you don't try to force it. The pins aren't very strong and if you bend one by hurrying, it might break when you try to straighten it. I once spent three hours soldering up a new end on a monitor cable; the density of the pins requires a thin soldering iron and steadier hands than mine. Some new video cards only have DVI (digital) connectors, but a simple converter for $10 will allow you to plug in an analog monitor. Only plasma screens and some LCD monitors are currently equipped for straight-through DVI cables.

Figure 3.12
Connecting the monitor

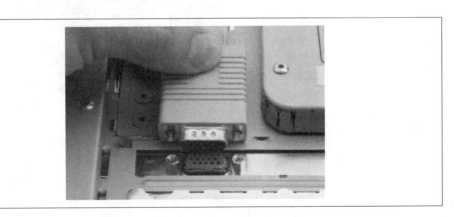

The external speakers are connected to the sound card through the speaker jack. The connection is a normal ministereo jack, which has three contact areas: left channel, right channel, and ground. The line jack is for unamplified audio and the mic jack allows you to record your own voice or do speech recognition. The 15-pin port on the sound card is for attaching a joystick. High-end sound systems featuring six-channel or eight-channel sound may require you to select the functionality of the audio ports in software.

Figure 3.13
Connecting
the speakers

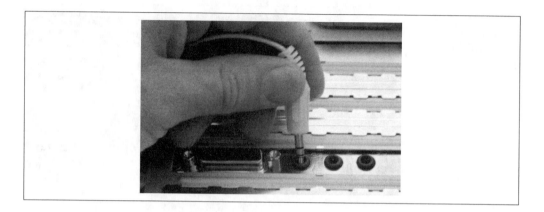

The modem port labeled "line" is connected to the phone jack on your wall, using the phone cable that comes with the modem. If you have a telephone connected to the wall jack, you can reconnect it to the phone port on the modem. The telephone will work whether the computer is on or off, providing the line isn't in use by the modem or another extension.

Figure 3.14
Connecting
the modem

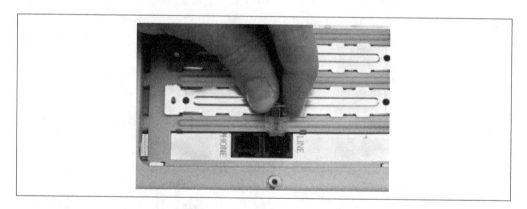

The PC, monitor, and any other peripherals attached to the PC should be plugged in to a common power strip with a surge protector. The common ground will eliminate the possibility of ground current loops.

Chapter 4

Building a Pentium 4 LGA in a Midtower Case

Step 1: Preparing the Case

The Antec case we chose for our build was purchased from our local CompUSA store, where a variety of cases were featured with the side panel removed to display the internal features. However, some of the nicest features are only obvious with the side panel installed, namely the thumb screws for opening the case and the combination locking/alignment tab. To the right of the thumb screw being removed in the picture is the protruding tab with a hole that can be padlocked to prevent component removal if the system is used in a public area.

Figure 4.1
Removing the side cover thumb screw

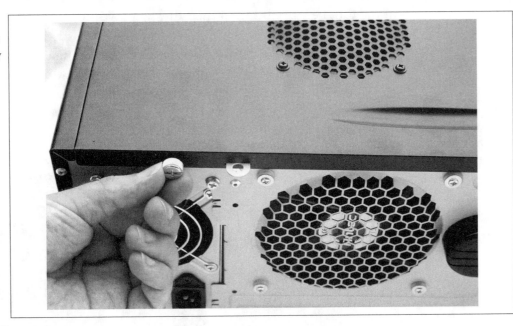

After removing the thumb screws and sliding the case cover straight back using the finger groove also visible in the previous picture, we need to remove the front facade. Front facades are not all removable; you have to inspect the inside of the case along the front to see if there's an obvious attachment mechanism. In this case, the facade is locked in by a series of plastic latching tabs along both edges. Each latch is disengaged from the case by pushing it out towards the edge of the case.

Figure 4.2
Disengaging a
front facade latch

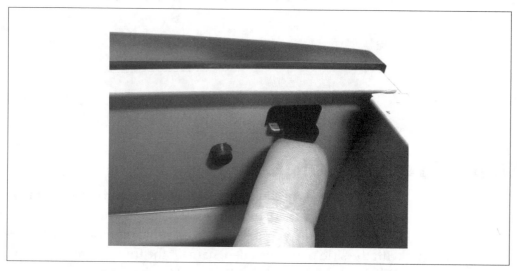

As each latching tab is freed, lift the facade away from the case at the bottom. Removable front facades are always lifted off from the bottom and pivot at the top, because doing it the other way would run into interference from any installed 5.25" drives. Lift the facade slowly and stop at any sign of resistance, since you've either missed the next tab, or the wires from the front facade LEDs and buttons are hung up in the case.

Figure 4.3
Removing the
front facade

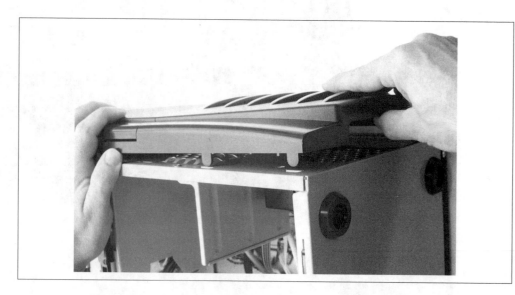

With the front facade removed, the four 5.25" bays at the top of the midtower are revealed. The Antec case uses an ingenious screwless rail system for mounting drives, with one snap-on rail used for each drive. We remove the snap-on rail, which is conveniently stored on the metal bay shield, and then we work the blank back and forth until the metal tongues fatigue and it breaks free. The purpose of these metal shields is to prevent radio frequency noise from escaping the case, so don't remove any more blanks than you have drives to install. After removing the shield, reinstall the front facade.

Figure 4.4
Breaking out the
5.25" bay shield

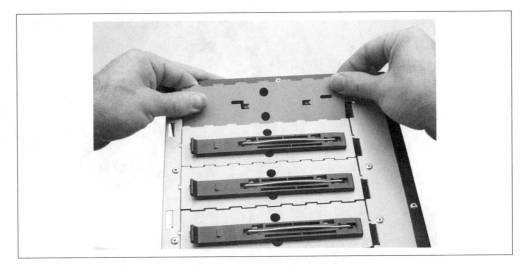

The case came with a 120 mm fan installed to exhaust hot air through the back of the case. Standard case fans are only 80 mm, and you'll often see room for two 80 mm rear exhaust fans in cases that don't employ a 120 mm fan. The following figure shows the 80 mm muffin fan we are preparing to install in the front of the case next to the 120 mm exhaust fan for comparison.

Figure 4.5
80 mm fan and
120 mm fan

Fans aren't sold as intake fans or exhaust fans. Fans only blow in one direction, so the function depends on which way you face the fan when you install it. Most cases come either with a front intake fan installed or with some form of snap-in fan mounting. This case provided a snap-in fan enclosure for the front that doubles as a guide for long adapter cards. We install the fan in the enclosure, making sure the label will face into the case.

Figure 4.6
Installing the
front intake fan

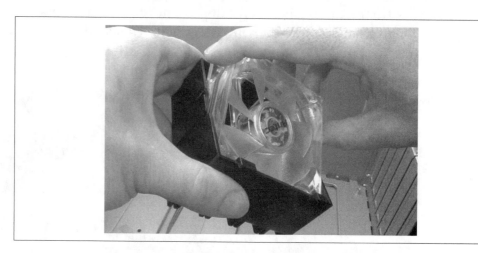

The intake fan enclosure pivots on the bottom edge and snaps into the place at the top. Note that the label on the fan motor is facing the inside of the case, so it will function as an intake fan. Also note that we routed the wires for the fan through the center of the enclosure so they won't get pinched. Including the fan of the CPU heatsink, the fan on the video adapter, and the power supply fan, we end up with a total of five cooling fans in this build.

Figure 4.7
Mounting
the intake
fan enclosure

The final step in preparing our Antec case for building is to remove the plastic accessory holder that covers the adapter slots. For an example of a locking rail used to secure the adapters, see our Athlon 64 build in Chapter 5. The plastic accessory holder doesn't contribute to securing the adapters, but when we reinstall it in Figure 4-53, you'll see the storage compartment in the holder that's accessible from the back of the case. The open space created above the slots makes it easier to install the adapters.

Figure 4.8
Removing the
adapter slots cover

Step 2: Installing the CPU

The motherboard for our Pentium 4 560 build is an Intel D925XCV. This was one of the first motherboards to support the LGA (Land Grid Array) version of the Pentium 4, in addition to introducing PCI Express 16X as a replacement for the long-standard AGP video. We install both the CPU and the memory before mounting the motherboard in the case. The PCI Express slots are black, so they don't show up as clearly as the white PCI conventional slots in the figure, but the forefinger in the picture is pointing out the sole PCI Express 16X slot, and the thumb is on one of the two PCI Express 1X slots.

Figure 4.9
PCI Express slots

The first step to installing the LGA version of the Pentium 4 is to remove the protective cover from the CPU Socket. Since Socket 775 consists of pins rather than holes, it could be irreparably damaged if something bashed or bent in a number of pins. The plastic cover is picked up on the end with the word "remove" stamped on it, and then lifted away from the socket.

Figure 4.10
Removing the protective cover from Socket 775

Next we lift the load lever by pulling it slightly away from the socket wall to disengage from the plastic ear, and then lift it well past the vertical and let it down at the end of its travel. The load lever is several times beefier than locking levers on recent CPU sockets, because it has to compress the spring steel of the load plate after the CPU is installed.

Figure 4.11
Lifting the load lever

The load plate is unique to the LGA CPU, which is pressed down on the contact legs in the socket. Previous PGA (Pin Grid Array) designs have the CPU pins seat in the socket holes, and the locking lever only functioned to lock the pins into place. The load plate is lifted up, a little past the vertical, where it stops and should remain in place.

Figure 4.12
Lifting the CPU retention bracket

There's a little gold triangle on one corner of the CPU package that matches the pin 1 corner of the socket. The CPU is aligned by two keys in the socket and two notches towards one side of the CPU package, so it can only sit flush in the socket when inserted properly. Make sure you have a good hold on the CPU as you lower it into the socket, because the CPU could damage the landing pins if it gets dropped on a steep angle.

Figure 4.13
Seating the Pentium 4 on the landing pins

Once our 3.6 GHz Pentium 4 is sitting level in the socket and you can plainly see the two notches in the CPU package are filled with the socket keys, lower the load plate until it sits loosely on the top of the CPU package. Now bring the load lever back up through the vertical and lower it until you can snap it under the stub holder on the side of the socket. Lowering the lever takes a bit of force because you are compressing the load plate, which in turn forces the CPU down tightly on the landing pins.

Figure 4.14
Locking the
Pentium 4
into place

Next we apply the thermal compound supplied with our Intel heatsink to the CPU. The instructions that came with the heatsink actually suggested we "mound" the thermal compound on the center of the CPU, which is what we did. Note this is in sharp contrast with many older types of heatsink/socket combinations that require just a drop of thermal grease. The small holes for the heatsink fasteners are visible less than an inch from each corner of the socket.

Figure 4.15
Applying
thermal
compound
to the CPU

The evaluation heatsink-assembly Intel supplied shipped with a protective plastic film over the copper core of the heatsink. The fan wiring needs to be routed right through the heatsink fins (the wires are protected by a high-temperature insulation) and pulled out the bottom, so it doesn't interfere with the fan. The left hand in the picture is holding the wires in place as the right hand peels off the plastic film.

Figure 4.16
Preparing the heatsink for installation

As the heatsink is lowered over the CPU, make sure the wires don't get pinched underneath. The heatsink should be lowered straight down on the CPU, but we're showing it on a tilt here so we don't completely obscure the socket. There is a white snap-in fastener on each corner of the heatsink, and four matching holes in the motherboard.

Figure 4.17
Heatsink shown over Socket 775

Once the snap-in fasteners on each corner of the heatsink are matched with the holes in the motherboard, simply push down on each black fastener cap until it clicks into place. The only trick is to lift up the motherboard a little so there's room for the connector to go through the hole. Flip the motherboard over when you're done and make sure the fasteners are fully engaged.

Figure 4.18
Securing the
heatsink fasteners

As soon as the heatsink is properly installed, connect the power for the heatsink fan to the designated fan connector on the motherboard. The connector is usually located right of the edge of the motherboard next to the CPU socket, but make sure the printing on the motherboard or the accompanying manual identifies it as the CPU fan point. This allows the BIOS to monitor the health of the fan and control its activity in power management modes.

Figure 4.19
Connecting the
heatsink fan

Step 3: Installing DDR-2 RAM

The first step to installing RAM in any motherboard is to consult the manual to determine the allowable configurations for the memory modules you have on hand. In this case, we'll be installing a matched pair of 512 MB DIMMs in dual-channel configuration. Once you determine which memory sockets to populate, open the white latches on both ends of the sockets.

Figure 4.20
Opening the
DIMM socket
latches

The notch near the center of the edge connector on the memory module must be aligned with the key in the socket for the module to fit. Because the notch is so near the center, you may choose the wrong orientation (there are only two possibilities). Hold the DIMM as close to the socket as you can get it to check you have it facing the right direction.

Figure 4.21
Checking the
socket key
alignment

The large number of spring contacts in memory sockets provide a good deal of resistance to inserting a DIMM. The 240 contacts on DDR-2 DIMMs may be a smaller than the 184 contacts on the standard DDR DIMM, but it feels like it takes more force to seat a DDR-2 DIMM. Push down evenly with a thumb on each end of the DIMM until the white latches raise to the closed position.

Figure 4.22
Seating the first
Crucial DDR2-533
DIMM

The second memory module is installed in the DIMM 0 socket of Channel B, to work in dual-channel mode with the first memory module, which was installed in DIMM 0 socket of Channel A. The latest Intel technology allows for interleaving DIMMs in dual-channel mode, which means if we had built the PC with two 256 MB DDR-2 modules, we could upgrade the amount to a full 1 GB with an odd number of DIMMs. This motherboard would allow us to use the original DIMMs together in Channel A, populate Channel B with a single 512 MB DIMM, and still operate in dual-channel mode.

Figure 4.23
Seating the second
Crucial DDR2-533
DIMM

Step 4: Installing the Motherboard

The first step to installing our motherboard is to remove the standard I/O core shield that shipped with our case and replace it with the custom shield that matches the motherboard I/O core. Some standard I/O shields are stamped out of the same metal as the back of the case, as in our Chapter 5 build. This standard I/O shield is a separate piece held in place by the spring force of the folded metal strips along the edges of the shield. A screwdriver serves to help compress the spring along one edge, after which the shield can be pushed down into the case.

Figure 4.24
Removing the standard I/O shield

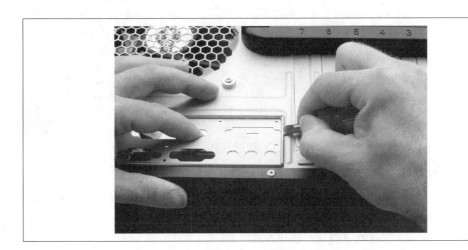

The custom I/O shield is now installed in the opening from the inside of the case. The symbols identifying the I/O ports face the outside of the case, and any grounding or positioning tabs above the port holes face the inside of the case. The two round port holes for the keyboard and the mouse go next to the power supply. The I/O shield is simply pressed into the opening, where spring force keeps it in place.

Figure 4.25
Installing the custom I/O shield

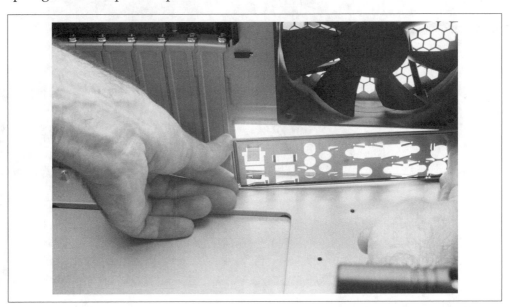

Some cases ship with a number of brass standoffs preinstalled in standard mounting positions, but this doesn't mean they will line up with the holes in your motherboard. Place the motherboard next to the case, and install standoffs in the predrilled holes in the case where it looks like they'll match holes in the motherboard. Count all of the installed standoffs, but do not tighten them at this point.

Figure 4.26
Screwing standoffs into the motherboard by hand

Next we test-fit the motherboard in the case, lowering it down onto the standoffs with two hands, and then easing towards the back of the case until the I/O core is in position through the I/O shield. To avoid dragging the motherboard on the standoffs during this operation, I usually lift a little on one of the white PCI slots and on the motherboard edge towards the front of the case. Now inspect the solder-ringed holes in the motherboard and make sure there's a brass standoff under each. If you have trouble determining this, shining a flashlight through the holes or under the motherboard can help.

Figure 4.27
Fitting the motherboard in the case

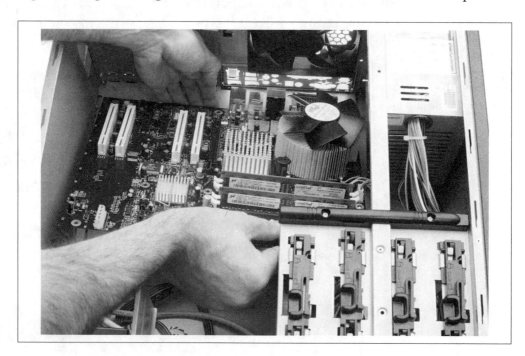

Next, remove the motherboard again, take out any standoffs that didn't align with holes, and then tighten the remaining standoffs. You can use a nut driver, socket, adjustable wrench, or even pliers; just make sure you don't create any brass splinters, or clean them up if you do. A fraction of a turn is all it takes to tighten a standoff. Count the standoffs, reinstall the motherboard, and install a screw in each ringed hole. If the screw count doesn't match the standoff count, you're going to have to remove the motherboard again and recount.

Figure 4.28
Tightening the
motherboard
screws

Double-check that the I/O core is fully engaged through the I/O shield, and that none of the metal tabs have been folded over any port openings. The I/O core of this Intel D925XCV motherboard includes all the standard I/O ports, plus a Gigabit Ethernet port, four USB 2.0 ports, a FireWire port, and optical and coax S/PDIF ports. Five audio out ports are present for the integrated eight-channel (7.1) sound.

Figure 4.29
Fully engaged
I/O core

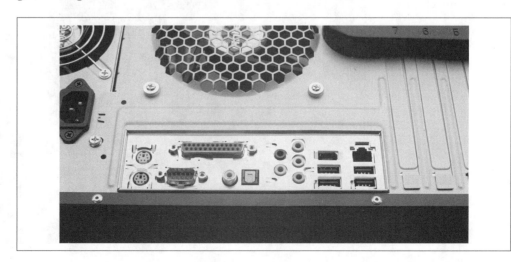

Step 5: Making Motherboard Connections

The most important step in making motherboard connections is to consult the manual that shipped with the motherboard. There are two options for powering this motherboard: one uses the standard ATX 20-wire connector, the other uses the 24-wire ATXe connector borrowed from the world of PC servers. The 24-wire receptacle on this particular Intel motherboard accepts the 20-pin connector, and it's keyed so it can only be inserted in the proper location, to one end of the receptacle.

Figure 4.30
Inserting the 20-wire ATX power

In addition to the standard 20-wire ATX power connector, most recent motherboards require an additional 12V connection. This is implemented as a square 4-wire connector that is normally located near the CPU. The connector is keyed so that it can only be inserted in the proper orientation.

Figure 4.31
Making the 12V power connection

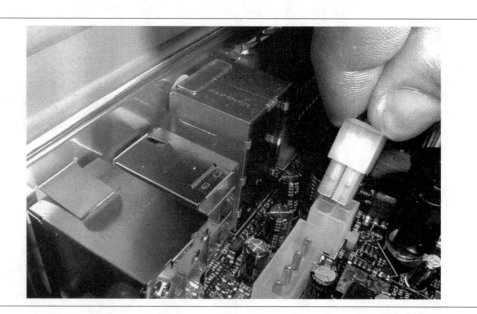

Finally, we need to do a "make up" connection, to compensate for the fact that we used a 20-wire instead of a 24-wire connector for the main motherboard power. You can buy an adapter that turns a 20-wire connector into a 24-wire connector, but if the power supply circuit doesn't provide sufficient power, it won't help. The motherboard provides an extra receptacle for a 1×4 power supply lead, which is located right next to the 12V connector on this motherboard.

Figure 4.32
Installing the alternate 1×4 power connector

Some power supplies can vary the fan speed for enhanced cooling or decrease the speed for quiet operation. In order for the BIOS to monitor the fan speed, the power supply must have a external fan connector that can be attached to the motherboard. Since this connection is for information only, the fan doesn't draw power from the connector and it may only use one wire. This can be attached to the auxiliary or back fan connection point.

Figure 4.33
Attaching the power supply fan monitoring lead

The large 120 mm exhaust fan that came preinstalled in our Antec case is powered by a 1×4 connector from the power supply. Since we already brought a power supply lead to the back of the case for the auxiliary power, the second connector on the lead makes a convenient power point for the fan.

Figure 4.34
Providing power to the rear exhaust fan

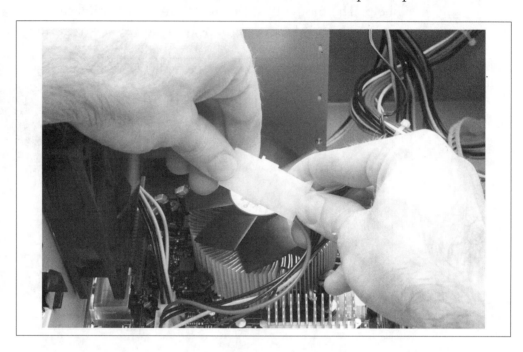

With such a large number of power supply leads routed between the rear exhaust fan and the CPU heatsink and fan, it's necessary to secure them out of the way where they won't interfere with the fans or be in danger of insulator degradation due to contact with heatsink fins. We bundle all the loose leads together and cable-tie them to the exhaust fan frame.

Figure 4.35
Bundling the power supply leads

The power lead for the front intake fan attaches to the front fan point on the motherboard. The 80 mm fan was equipped with a 1×4 adapter for direct connection to the power supply if a motherboard connection point wasn't available, but in this case, we're more likely to run out of power supply leads than motherboard fan connectors.

Figure 4.36
Attaching the power for the intake fan

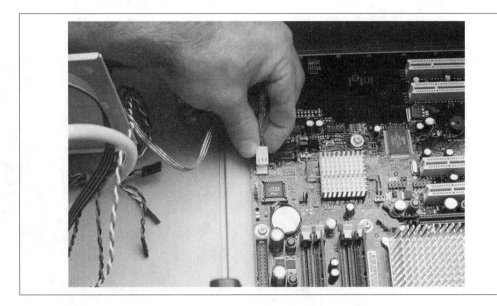

The most important connection from the front panel to the motherboard is the power switch, without which the PC can't be turned on. Depending on the motherboard and the case manufacturer, some of the front panel leads may be color coded, or even bundled into semi-standard block connectors. The functions of the front panel leads are printed right on the connectors, but the motherboard labeling may be cryptic or even absent, so have the manual at hand, or print the necessary pages if the manual only exists as a PDF on the driver CD.

Figure 4.37
Connecting the front panel power switch

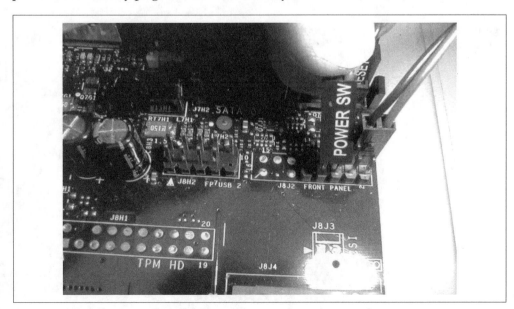

Front panel LED leads installed backwards won't operate, but won't do any harm, while switches will work as long as they go on the correct two posts. Most new cases feature front panel USB and audio ports, and in this instance, the connector for the front two USB ports is integrated into a single cable and keyed to be installed in the proper orientation.

Figure 4.38
Connecting
the front panel
USB ports

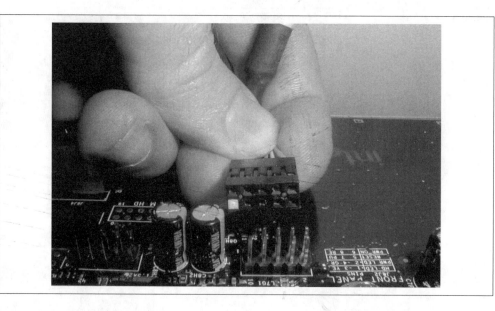

Step 6: Installing a Two-Drive Array

We assemble and install our two-drive SATA array at this point for the simple reason that the drive cage can't be removed once the PCI Express video adapter is installed. The 3.5" drive cage is supported and secured by metal guides and a locking lever. The locking lever is pushed towards the inside of the case, and the whole cage slides out horizontally with very little resistance.

Figure 4.39
Removing the
3.5" drive cage

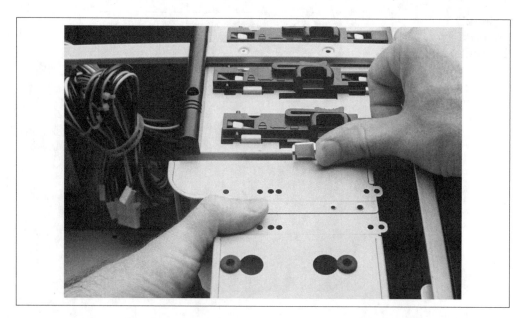

We'll be installing two 3.5" Seagate Barracuda SATA hard drives, 200 GB each, for a total array capacity of 400 GB. There are two bays in the cage equipped with shock absorbing rubber mounts, which help protect the hard drives from vibrations in the case. In order to use the bays with the shock absorbing mounts, the drives can only be installed in one orientation; the screw holes won't line up any other way.

Figure 4.40
Installing the first
Seagate Barracuda
drive in the cage

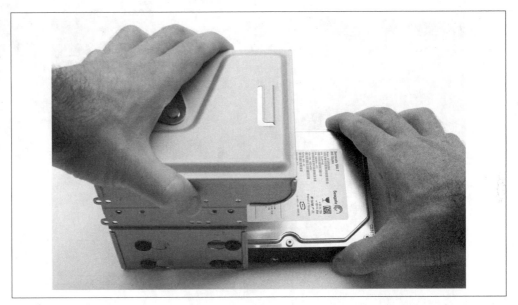

The drive is secured with four special screws that were supplied with the case hardware. Overtightening the screws would simply crush the rubber mounts, so don't run the screws in with all your strength. One of the screws with its unthreaded upper shaft is shown sitting on the side of the hard drive to the left of the screwdriver.

Figure 4.41
Securing the
hard drive

The second hard drive is installed in the cage right above the first. The advantage of the removable drive cage is that the drives can be aligned and secured with screws on both sides without having to access the other side of the case. The top two bays in the cage could be used for a floppy drive and another 3.5" drive, but we won't be installing either in this build.

Figure 4.42
Installing the
second Seagate
Barracuda hard
drive

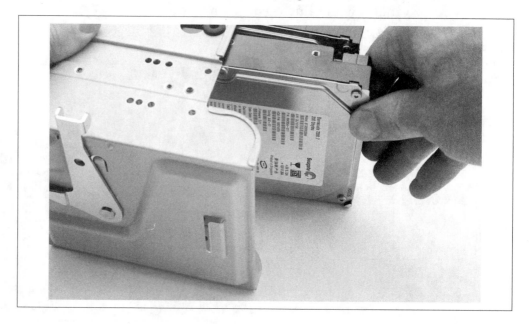

With both drives installed in the shock absorbing bays of the drive cage, you can see that there's a small air space between them. The drives do not touch each other. A tower case, like that used in our Chapter 6 build, has multiple removable drive cages that allow for greater drive spacing.

Figure 4.43
Securing the
second drive
with four screws

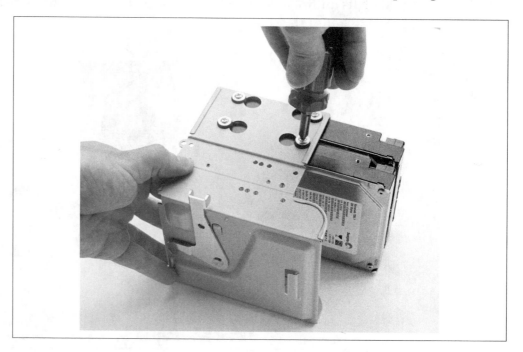

The drive cage is reinstalled in the case infrastructure by sliding it in on the horizontal. This means there must be an open space in the case as deep as the length of the hard drives, which is why we had to install the drives before the video adapter.

Figure 4.44
Sliding the cage into the case infrastructure

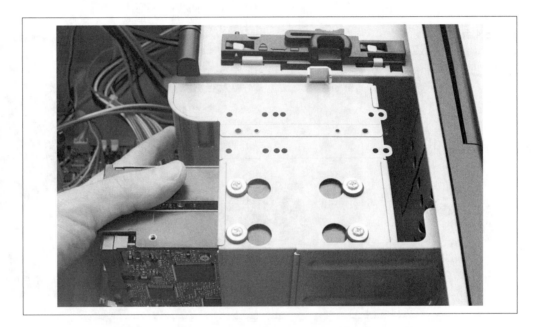

While the drive cage is supported in the vertical plane by the case infrastructure as soon as it's slid into place, it will still slide in the horizontal plane until you close the locking lever. The lever should operate with very little resistance. If it seems to be bound, remove the cage again and make sure it actually slid in properly on the guides.

Figure 4.45
Locking the drive cage into place

Next we install our SATA power connectors on the drives. This is another step that we are taking now simply because it would be very difficult to carry it out once the video adapter is installed. The two SATA power connectors are fit on the larger edge connectors of the hard drive, and they are keyed so they can only be installed in the proper orientation.

Figure 4.46
Installing the SATA power connectors

Newer power supplies are starting to ship with SATA power connectors as standard option, but most existing power supplies require a simple adapter. In this case, we used an SATA power adapter, two connectors located on a 4-wire cable bundle, which is then connected to a standard 1×4 connector from the power supply.

Figure 4.47
Connecting the SATA power adapter to a power supply lead

Step 7: Installing Adapters

The Nvidia GeForce 6800 PCI Express 16X video adapter has an onboard programmable graphics processor, and is equipped with a large heatsink and cooling fan. In order to ensure that the adapter gets sufficient power, it requires a direct connection to the power supply. The video adapter was shipped with a custom power adapter, which in turn is connected to a standard 1×4 power supply lead, just like our SATA power adapter in Figure 4-47.

Figure 4.48
Attaching the custom power adapter to the video adapter

The PCI Express 16X adapter is installed in the sole matching slot on the motherboard. There is a locking mechanism to help keep the adapter seated in the slot, though it's not the full lock that's commonly used on AGP slots. The little black locking tab is being pushed out by the finger to the lower right of the mermaid, while the adapter is seated in the slot with even pressure from both hands.

Figure 4.49
Installing the Nvidia GeForce PCI Express video adapter

Make sure the video ports are all fully exposed through the rear of the case, and secure it in place with a screw. This model of the Nvidia GeForce adapter sports two digital video monitor connectors (DVI) and an S-video port, but not a single standard VGA port. A simple DVI to VGA adapter allows you to run a monitor with an analog connector, including most older LCDs, on this video card. Large plasma displays and newer LCDs are generally equipped with DVI connectors, or both types.

Figure 4.50
Securing the
video adapter

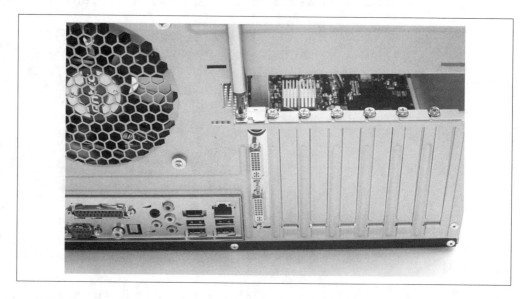

We installed a V.92 modem in the bottom PCI slot, as far as possible from the video adapter, which needs room for the cooling fan to be effective. The modem is seated in the slot with even pressure on both ends, which is made easy thanks to the opening in the back of the case above the adapter mounting area.

Figure 4.51
Installing a V.92
PCI voice modem

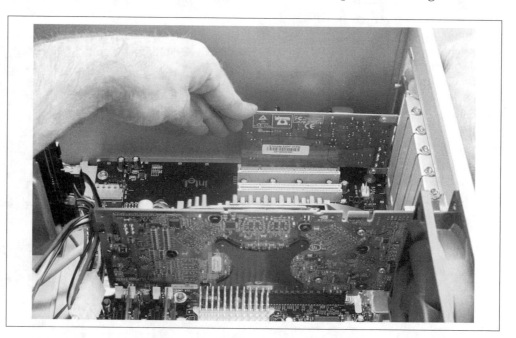

The line and phone ports on the modem take up nearly the whole width of the slot opening, so it's important to make sure the full port is exposed before securing the adapter with a screw. While it's easy to get a phone jack into a port even if it's a little off-center, it's impossible to get it out again without straightening the modem.

Figure 4.52
Securing the modem

The final step to installing the adapters is to replace the plastic slots cover. It hinges on the right side and snaps into place on the left, where the release latch extends into the case. You can see the raised lettering of the Hardware compartment, a handy place to store any leftover screw when the build is complete.

Figure 4.53
Reinstalling the adapter slots cover

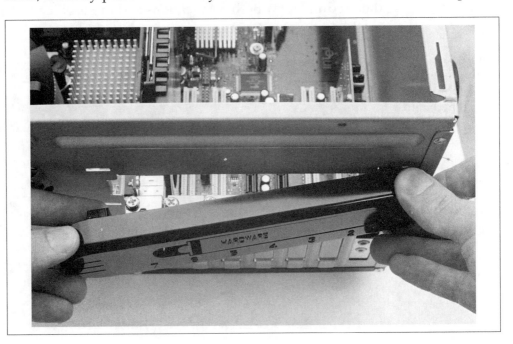

Step 8: Finishing the Hard Drive Array

Now that the video adapter has been installed, we can continue with the final connections on our drive array. The SATA data cable is a smaller format connector than the SATA power cable, and each drive requires its own cable for the point-to-point connection. The cable connector is keyed so it can only be mated in the correct orientation.

Figure 4.54
Connecting an
SATA data cable
to the hard drive

There are four Serial ATA connection points on our motherboard, which also support RAID 0 and RAID 1 configurations. RAID 0 supports drive striping, which increases the overall array performance by working the drives in parallel, and RAID 1 mirrors the drives, making an exact copy for data redundancy. Both applications require a pair of identical drives. The motherboard SATA connection is also keyed for proper mating.

Figure 4.55
Connecting the
SATA cable to
the motherboard

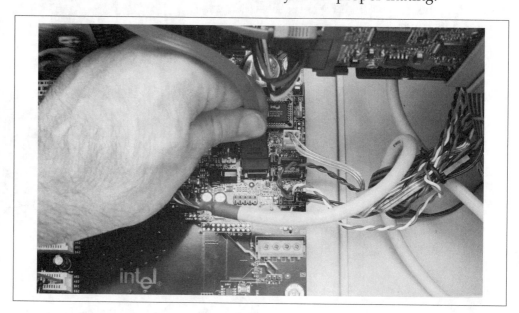

Our second drive in the array is connected the same as the first, though we had to be careful not to stress the edge connector on the drive due to physical interference from the video adapter. The edge connector can be damaged by excessive force, so you need to be a little careful working around any SATA connectors. The other end of the cable is attached to another SATA connector on the motherboard.

Figure 4.56
Connecting the
second SATA
data cable

You can see from the following picture that cable manufacturers tend to err on the side of making SATA cables too long. Keeping in mind the somewhat fragile edge connectors, we cable-tied the slack to keep it from creating a pulling hazard. The finger at the bottom of the picture is pointing to a white latch on a DIMM socket. The long video adapter obstructs the latches so that no memory can be installed or removed with the video adapter in place.

Figure 4.57
Bundling the
SATA data cables

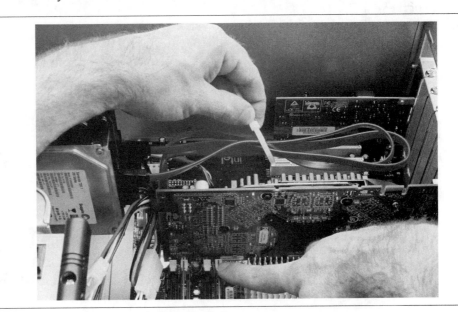

Since all 5.25" drives are installed from the front of the case, it's necessary to remove the plastic blank for whichever bays are being used. This blank is held in place by a little plastic latch on the right-hand side. Cheaper cases usually require you to pop out the blanks from the inside.

Figure 4.58
Removing the plastic 5.25" bay blank

Step 9: Installing the DVD Recorder

Our Antec case features a screwless rail system for mounting the 5.25" drives. The two wire stubs protruding from the black plastic rail are actually opposite ends of a long stiff wire that acts as a spring.

Figure 4.59
Wire ends of the screwless rail

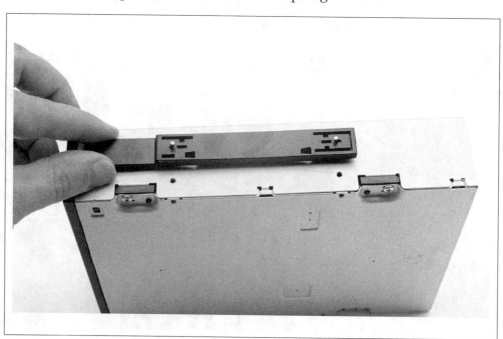

By holding the drive up to the open bay, we determine that the rail needs to be attached to the bottom set of holes in the side of the drive. Hook one end of the wire into one of the holes, and then push down on the center of the exposed length of wire, which acts as a spring. The other end of the wire should click into place and lock the rail firmly to the drive unless you pry it off.

Figure 4.60
Snapping the screwless rail into place

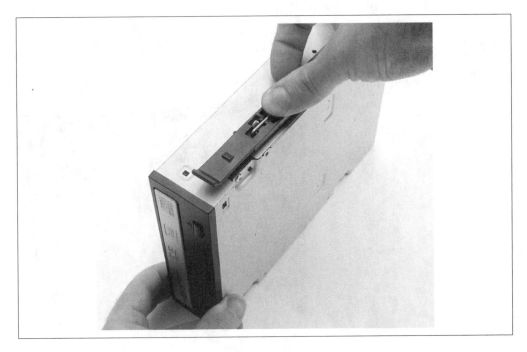

Before installing the DVD recorder in the case, we attach the CD Audio connector. It's easier to make this attachment at this point because once installed, it will be against the side of the case with plenty of power supply cables in the way. The white jumper to the right of the audio connector is the Master/Slave jumper, which is set to Master.

Figure 4.61
Connecting the CD Audio lead to the DVD recorder

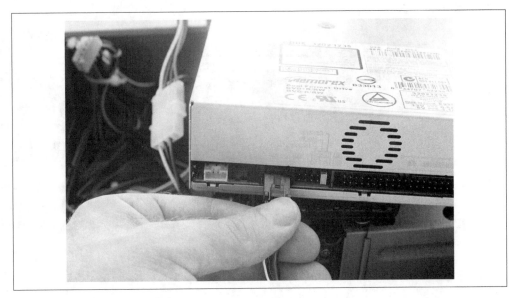

The drive is then slid into position from the front of the case. If you're building a system with multiple DVD or CD drives sharing a cable, you'll have to choose one drive to be Master and one drive to be Slave, and set the corresponding jumper on the back of the drive. It's very rare these days to share an IDE ribbon cable between an optical drive and a parallel IDE hard drive because of the degradation in hard drive performance.

Figure 4.62
Installing the Memorex DVD recorder

The drive is held in place by sliding the plastic lock on the side of the bay towards the back of the case. If you forget this step, you'll notice the drive moving when you go to install the power connector.

Figure 4.63
Locking the DVD recorder into place

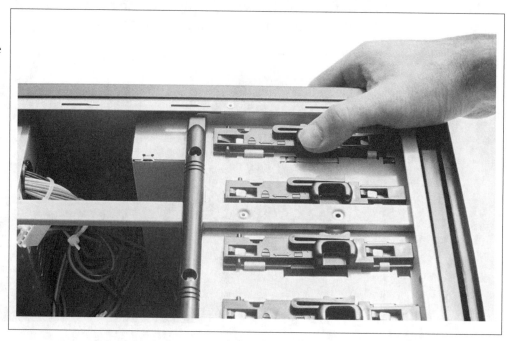

Next we attach the other end of the CD audio cable to the proper connection point on the motherboard. It's a good idea to check the manual if the motherboard doesn't have a clearly labeled CD in or CD Audio port. The lock on the connector serves as a key to prevent it from being inserted backwards. In some builds, you'll have to connect the CD audio cable before you install all of the adapters because they will block access to the port.

Figure 4.64
Connecting the
CD audio cable to
the motherboard

Next we connect the 40-wire parallel IDE cable to the DVD recorder. There's no advantage to using 80-wire IDE cables with DVD and CD drives; the old 40-wire cables provide more than enough bandwidth for their relatively slow transfer speeds. The cable header is keyed so it only fits into the drive with the colored key wire on pin 1.

Figure 4.65
Connecting the
IDE cable to the
DVD recorder

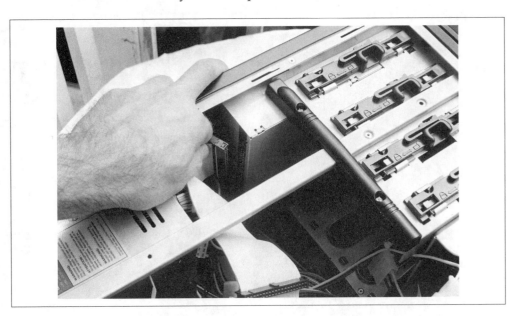

There's only a single IDE controller on this motherboard, with four SATA ports. They don't expect anybody to install older technology hard drives. The IDE controller is located on the edge of the motherboard, next to the floppy controller, which we didn't use in this build. The cable is keyed to fit one way, but it doesn't hurt to confirm that the colored key wire is to the pin 1 end of the connector, sometimes marked with an arrow or a spot.

Figure 4.66
Connecting the
IDE cable to the
controller

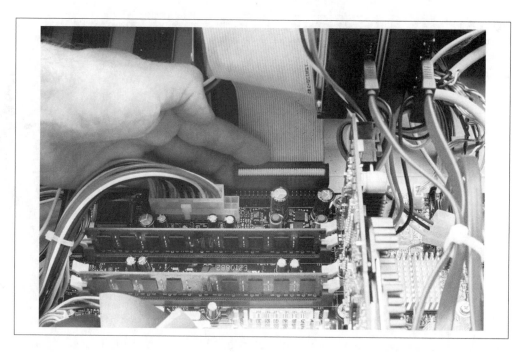

The final step to connecting up our DVD recorder is to connect the power. The 1×4 connector from the power supply is rounded on two corners so it can only be inserted the right way, but it takes a bit of pushing. You don't have to get it seated all the way to the ridge stop, just far enough so it doesn't pull out easily.

Figure 4.67
Connecting
power to the
DVD recorder

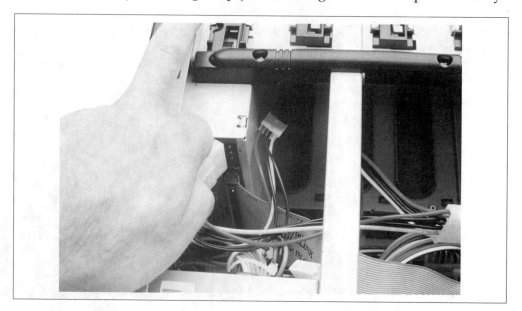

Step 10: Closing Up and CMOS Setup

Before closing up the case, lift it a few inches off the table, and tilt it slowly back and forth, listening for any loose screws rolling around. If you hear something suspicious, stop and find out what it is. As we replace the side cover on our Antec midtower, you can see the special circular hood that gets positioned over the CPU heatsink fan, giving it a direct path to outside air through the side. The side cover is secured with two thumbscrews.

Figure 4.68
CPU heatsink
fan hood

After we hook up the basic I/O devices, monitor and power (see Chapter 3), we're ready to enter CMOS Setup and configure our hardware. The main setup screen shows our Pentium 4 560 at 3.6 GHz, and correctly identifies the memory speed as 533 MHz (PC2-4300). The memory mode is dual channel, and the Slot 0 of both channels A and B location is populated with a 512 MB DDR-2 module.

Figure 4.69
Main screen in the
BIOS Setup Utility

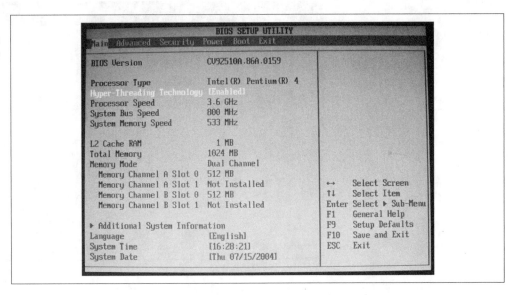

Most of the options for BIOS Setup are under the Advanced menu. The defaults are fine in most cases, though it's a good idea to take a look at each screen just to make sure you're getting what you expected. If you have trouble when you go to install the operating system, try changing the Boot Configuration to make the CD or DVD drive the first boot device.

Figure 4.70
Advanced options in the BIOS Setup Utility

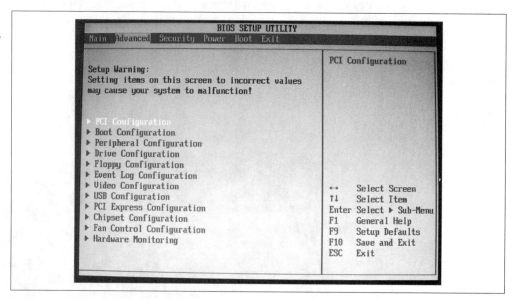

We chose to show the Drive Configuration screen, in part to show how terminology evolves over time. The Memorex DVD recorder is shown as the PATA Master, where PATA stands for Parallel ATA. We enabled the Intel RAID controller at this point, since we want to configure our drives in an array and the default setting was "disabled." See Chapter 6 for configuring a RAID. Note that we'll need to temporarily install a floppy drive to load the driver for Windows XP and make our RAID bootable.

Figure 4.71
Drive Configuration screen

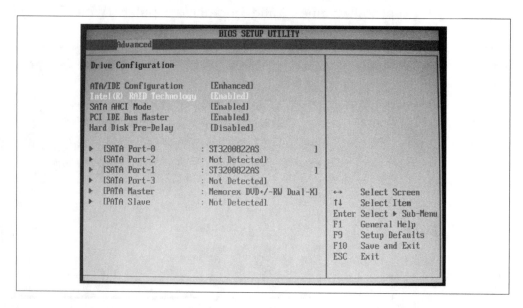

Our final stop in the BIOS Setup utility before saving and exiting is the Hardware Monitoring screen. It's always a good idea to stop on this screen for a few minutes to make sure that the CPU temperature reaches a plateau and stabilizes, and that the power supply voltages are stable. It's okay for a power supply voltage to flip back and forth between two values, which are approximations in any case, but it shouldn't wander through a whole series of different values.

Figure 4.72
Hardware
Monitoring screen

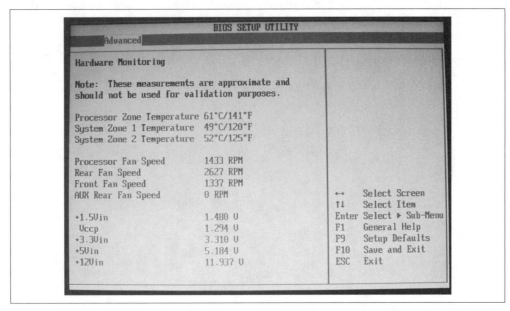

Chapter 5

Building an Athlon 64 or Athlon 64 FX in a Midtower Case

Step 1: Preparing the Case

We chose this small midtower case for its simple side-panel access and its use of a locking bar for the adapters. Unlike many midtower designs that hide the screws securing the side panels under the front facade or a top-hat cover, these screws were plainly visible from the back. Each side panel is secured with two screws right on the back edges of the case, and we begin by removing the "up" panel, the one that is on the right-hand side when you look at the case from the back. After the screws are removed, the panel slides back and comes away from the case.

Figure 5.1
Removing the side panel

Next we remove the locking bar from the adapter cage section of the case. The bar, really a three-dimensional sheet-metal construction, is held in place by a single screw. The screw is removed and we slide the locking bar up and set it aside. We'll illustrate the installation of the locking bar with a number of pictures after the adapters are installed.

Figure 5.2
Removing the locking bar

Unless your motherboard has very limited I/O capabilities, it will be sold with a custom ATX I/O shield to replace the basic one that ships with the case. On inexpensive cases, the shield is punched out of the same thin sheet metal as the rest of the case back. The punch leaves the shield connected by thin metal tongues at six points, which can be carefully clipped with thin wire cutters, or fatigued and broken off by flexing the shield. I always choose the latter approach, though you must be careful not to stretch or bend the sheet metal of the case itself, and you need to be cautious of burrs and jagged outcrops left around the opening. If you identify any sharp edges that look like they could slice your fingers, bend them over to the inside with big tweezers or small pliers.

Figure 5.3
Breaking out the standard I/O shield

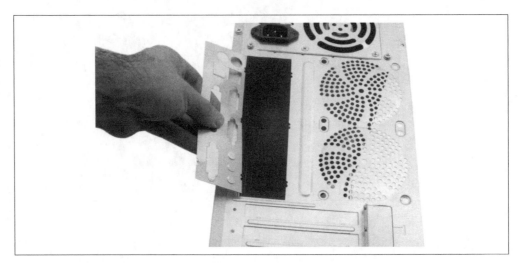

Sometimes, when you buy a case through mail order, as we did this one, you get an unpleasant surprise. We purchased this case specifically to illustrate the adapter locking bar, but the 350-watt power supply included with the case was very low quality. Don't put your trust in the sticker on power supplies—anybody can print stickers. So, while not part of the ideal build story, our next step is to remove the cheap power supply that shipped with the case, which is secured with four screws from the back of the case. To prevent the power supply from dropping into the case and causing damage, either do this with the case on its side or make sure you're holding the power supply with your other hand before taking out the last screw.

Figure 5.4
Removing the power supply

Standard ATX power supplies are all physically interchangeable, but the one that comes with your case may not have all the connectors you need. The standard power supply we purchased sported the extra Pentium 4 connectors, including the 12V header used by our Asus motherboard for the Athlon 64. We didn't purchase a power supply with the new SATA power connectors because we will be using the legacy power connectors in this build, but adapters to convert the old-fashioned power connectors for SATA were supplied with the motherboard. The extra intake fan on our replacement supply increases the airflow through the case, but it doesn't meet AMD's recommendation for an additional exhaust fan with the Athlon 64, so one of our final steps in this build will be to include an additional muffin fan. We install the power supply and secure it with the same four screws.

Figure 5.5
Installing the
replacement
power supply

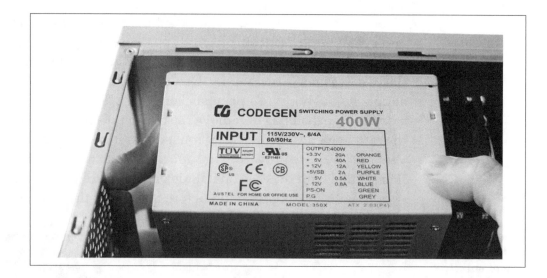

While the order of these preparatory steps isn't critical, I save installing the new I/O shield that comes with the motherboard for last, because they are often so flimsy they'll just keep popping out until the motherboard is installed. The shield snaps into place from the inside, with the two round holes for the keyboard and mouse connections closest to the power supply. Any projecting tabs should face the inside of the case, and any markings should be readable from the outside. If all three of these conditions are met, the shield will be installed in the proper orientation, though you'll get a chance to double-check when you test-fit the motherboard.

Figure 5.6
Installing the
custom I/O shield

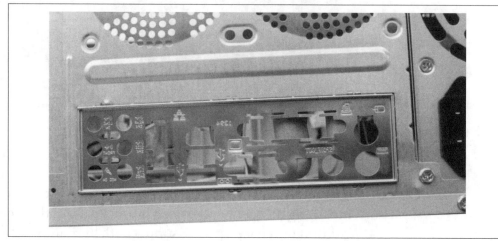

Step 2: Installing the CPU and Heatsink

Large CPUs, like our Athlon 64, require fairly massive heatsinks to prevent overheating and failure. You should never power up any modern motherboard and CPU combination without a heatsink installed, or the CPU will most likely be ruined. The mass of the heatsink is more than can be supported by the old method of latching it directly to the socket, so a special retention module is required. If your retention module is shipped with instructions that contradict those written here, follow the instructions that came with your specific model.

The backing plate of this retention module is mounted on the back of the motherboard, and two threaded standoffs for attaching the module framework project through special holes in the motherboard. The backing plate may already be installed on your motherboard when you purchase it. If not, remove the protective paper from the sticky coating that will hold the backing plate to the bottom of the motherboard, line up the threaded standoffs with the holes, and press it flat.

Figure 5.7
Installing the backing plate

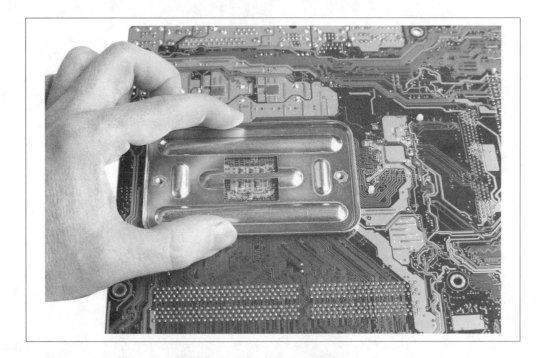

The retention module base is a light, plastic framework that provides two critical functions. First, it provides the stubs, or ears, that the spring clips on the heatsink will latch over. Second, the inside ledges of the base regulate the height of the heatsink over the CPU, a tiny fraction of an inch. Run in the two screws that hold the retention module base to the backing plate with your fingers, and then snug them up with a screwdriver. It's critical to install the retention module base properly because the spring force the retention bracket employs to lock the heatsink to the CPU is appreciable.

Figure 5.8
Tightening
the module
base screws

Raise the locking lever on the CPU socket to the vertical, or even a little further, if it goes easily. If the CPU is installed with the locking lever not fully opened, the CPU won't sit all the way down into the socket. This could easily result in damage to the CPU if the heatsink is installed over it and presses down too hard on the metal CPU cover.

Figure 5.9
Opening the
Socket 939
locking lever

There is a little gold triangle on both sides of one corner of the Athlon 64 module. That triangle matches with the triangle that appears on just one corner of the socket. The Athlon 64 3800+ CPU is shown lying on the socket upside down here, so you can see both the matching triangles and how the CPU legs patch the hole pattern in the socket.

Figure 5.10
Athlon 64 upside down on socket

Modern CPU sockets are all of the Zero Insertion Force (ZIF) type, so if the CPU doesn't drop right into the socket, make sure you have the orientation correct. The CPU only goes the one way, with the triangles matching up. If it still doesn't want to drop in, make sure the locking lever is still all the way up. If that doesn't do it, inspect the bottom of the CPU for any bent legs. The legs are very delicate and won't survive a lot of moving around, but you can usually straighten one or more legs by inserting a flat metal blade between two rows and gently pressing the bent leg(s) back in line with the others. As soon as the CPU is seated flat, lock it in place by lowering the locking lever until it clicks over the ear on the socket.

Figure 5.11
Locking the
CPU into place

Some heatsinks are sold with a preinstalled thermal interface covered with a sheet of contact paper, others come with a special tube of thermal grease, still others are shipped bare. Some form of thermal special compound between the CPU in the heatsink is required for proper cooling. In this instance, we applied a small drop of Arctic Silver 5, a polysynthetic silver compound. It's not necessary to spread the drop over the metal CPU cover or the heatsink. It will spread out over the area of the CPU die once the heatsink is installed.

Figure 5.12
Applying a drop
of Arctic Silver
thermal compound

This heatsink features a thick copper base for heat conduction, topped by cooling fins and a fan. It's definitely heavy enough to cause serious damage if you let it drop out of your hand and crash into the motherboard or CPU, so be a little careful. Line up the edges of the heatsink with the retention module, and then lower it into the retention module base. There's not a lot of room for movement once the heatsink is sitting in the retention module, but I give it a little wiggle just to encourage the thermal compound to start spreading evenly before the heatsink gets locked down.

Figure 5.13
Lowering the heatsink into the retention module base

You can only latch the clips over the ears on the retention module base one side at a time, and I like starting with the easy side, the side without the retention locking lever. It won't take much force to get the latch over the ear; it's just a matter of getting enough of the latch metal to project through that side of the heatsink and to line it up right.

Figure 5.14
Hooking the
first retention
latch over
the base

The latch on the other side of the heatsink needs to be pushed straight down to click in place over the ear on the housing base. If you have any trouble carrying out this operation, make sure the alignment is correct, that an even amount of the metal bracket is projecting from both sides of the heatsink, and that the other side is still latched in place. This shouldn't take a lot of force. You may even be able to do it with a forefinger instead of pushing with your thumb.

Figure 5.15
Latching the
second side
of the heatsink

The most physically challenging part of the heatsink installation is rotating the retention bracket lock clockwise to the locked position. The spring resistance is primarily in the first 2/3 of the turn, after which it goes through a tipping point and drops into place. If your thumb slips off the lever before the tipping point, it will snap back to its rest position with surprising force. Make sure you're holding the motherboard in place with your other hand so it doesn't slide off across the table as you rotate the lock.

Figure 5.16
Rotating the retention bracket lock

The final step with any heatsink installation is attaching the power lead for the heatsink fan to the proper power point on the motherboard. With any well-designed motherboard, this power point is right next to the CPU socket. Connecting the heatsink fan to the proper point allows for the BIOS to monitor the fan for failure and control the fan in advanced power management schemes.

Figure 5.17
Connecting the CPU heatsink fan to the proper power point

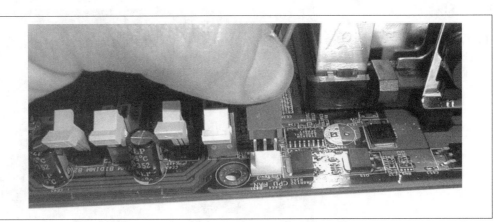

Step 3: Installing the Memory

The first step to installing a memory DIMM is to unlock the socket by spreading the levers on both sides. There are four DIMM sockets on our dual-channel Asus motherboard, two blue and two black. DIMM sockets of the same color must be populated by identical DIMMs, unless you're planning to operate the motherboard in single-channel mode (not recommended), in which case you would populate only the #1 blue socket.

Figure 5.18
Unlocking the
DIMM sockets

Line up the notch in the contact edge of the DIMM with the key in the socket you are populating. The DIMM is keyed to be inserted one way only; it will refuse to seat if you try forcing it in backwards, and may damage either the module or the socket. The metal casing on the DIMM with the Corsair labeling is retained with a wire spring and serves as a heat spreader for the memory chips.

Figure 5.19
Lining up
the DIMM
notch with
the socket key

Our system features two 512 MB DIMMs of DDR 400 memory, for 1 Giga-byte total installed. Seat the first DIMM with even pressure applied to both ends with your thumbs, and watch for the locking levers to rise into place as the DIMM seats. If the DIMM doesn't seat under the application of a steady pressure, double-check that the key is properly aligned with the socket and that the DIMM is approved for your motherboard.

Figure 5.20
Seating the
first DIMM

The second DIMM must be installed in the remaining blue socket. If we were installing four DIMMs, the next two would have to be a matched pair and would be installed in the black sockets. The second DIMM usually seats much easier than the first since you now have a feel for how much pressure is required on the particular motherboard.

Figure 5.21
Seating the
second DIMM

Step 4: Installing the Motherboard

The first step to installing the motherboard is to examine the case to make sure there are no obstructions or geometry problems to the motherboard fitting. Lay the motherboard flat next to the case, in the orientation it will be once it's installed. Next populate the motherboard pan (the metal case structure the motherboard will be mounted on) with brass standoffs in the predrilled holes that look like they'll line up with the holes in the motherboard, but do not tighten them.

Figure 5.22
Screwing in a brass standoff by hand

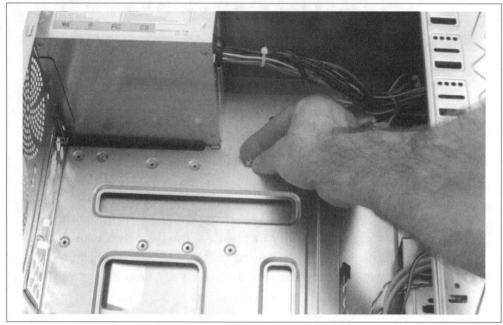

Next, test-fit the motherboard in the case to see if all of the brass standoffs line up with the holes in the motherboard. I usually lower the motherboard while holding onto the CPU heatsink and the PCI slots. Then, I let go of the heatsink and lift it off the standoffs from the front edge, to slide the I/O core into the I/O shield. In a tight case like this one, it pays to install the motherboard before the additional exhaust fan and the drives, or there's just no room to lower it into the case.

Figure 5.23
Test-fitting the
motherboard

Once you've confirmed that the motherboard fits properly and all of the standoffs are in the correct places, remove the motherboard again and set it aside. Now tighten all of the brass standoffs, either with a nutdriver or regular pliers, around a half a turn, depending on how much resistance they offer. They'll strip fairly easily, so don't try making them super tight, but on the other hand, you don't want them turning out if you need to remove the motherboard screws at a later date. Count out a number of screws that matches the number of standoffs and set them aside.

Figure 5.24
Tightening
the standoffs

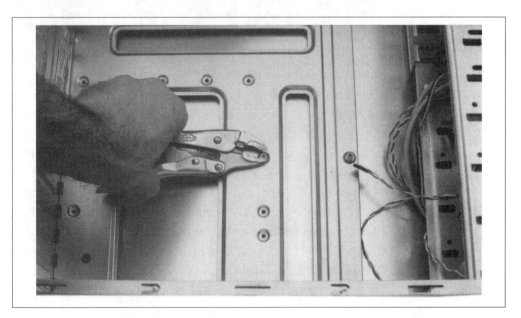

Next, reinstall the motherboard, and make sure the I/O shield doesn't pop out of place in the process. I usually start with the screw at the top, inside corner, because it helps hold the motherboard in place if the I/O shield is springy or if the case geometry is a little tweaked. Make sure you use every screw that you set aside in the previous step. If there's a screw left over when you're done, it means you either counted wrong or there's a standoff hidden under the motherboard waiting to cause a short circuit when you power up. You'll have to take the motherboard out again and remove the standoff that didn't line up with a hole.

Figure 5.25
Installing the
motherboard
screws

Inspect the I/O core from the back of the case to make sure that all the ports are accessible and that the shield is firmly in place. While it's a bit frustrating to have to remove the motherboard again at this point just to align the shield, it makes more sense to do it now than after you've made all the motherboard connections and installed the adapters. The functions of the six audio jacks on the right side of the I/O core are variable, controlled by the Realtek ALC850 software shipped with the motherboard. The motherboard can generate 4-channel, 6-channel, or 8-channel sound and supports the required cables by changing the functionality of the standard line-in, line-out, and mic-in ports. The I/O core also features optical and coax connectors for the Sony/Philips Digital Interface (S/PDIF), in addition to a Gigabit Ethernet connection, a multitude of USB ports, and a FireWire (IEEE 1394) port.

Figure 5.26
Inspecting
the I/O shield

Athlon 64 motherboards require two power connectors, the standard ATX connector and the additional 12V connector. The 12V connector is a simple, square four-wire connector that is usually located right next to the CPU. The locking latch generally faces into the center of the motherboard so you can get at it without removing the power supply if it becomes necessary to undo it for any reason. The plastic latch just springs into place as you insert the connector, which is keyed to fit one way only.

Figure 5.27
Inserting the
12V connector

The standard ATX power connector consists of two rows of ten wires, and is keyed to fit into the motherboard receptacle in the proper orientation. If you need to remove it for any reason, the latch is released by squeezing the top part back into the connector itself, which levers the bottom part open. It can take a bit of force to seat the connector, due to the size, so if the motherboard isn't well supported by standoffs on both sides of the connector, I work my fingertips under the edge of the board to support it. Just don't stick them way under or they'll either get stuck or punched full of little holes!

Figure 5.28
Making the ATX
power connection

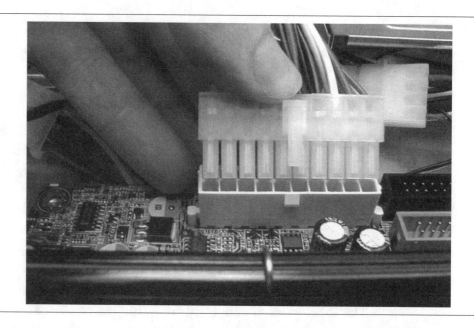

Our case came equipped with an intake fan at the bottom of the front facade. It's a good idea to make the power connection for any front-mounted
fans at this point, just so you don't forget later down the line. Many motherboards feature intake fan connection points, so they can be controlled by the
BIOS if the system features a "quiet" mode, but this requires that the fan feature a small format connector. This fan is powered by an inline connector that
goes on the end of one of the drive power leads.

Figure 5.29
Connecting the
intake fan power

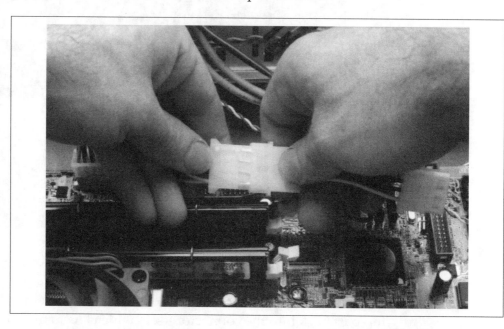

Despite the trend towards color coding everything on motherboards, I always check the documentation for the proper installation of front panel leads
to the motherboard, whenever available. The power switch, reset switch,

hard drive activity, and system power LEDs are normally included in the same block with the diagnostic speaker connection. The switches are nonpolarized; they work either way as long as they connect to the right posts, but the LEDs will only light up if the polarity is correct.

Figure 5.30
Connecting the front switches and LEDs

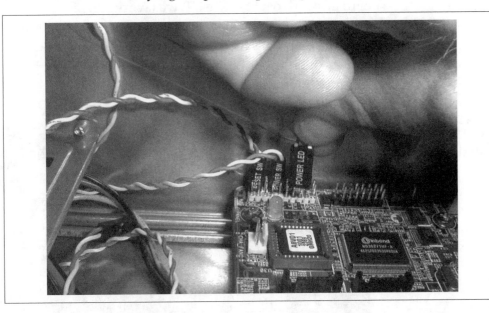

This case features a whole set of front connectors for user convenience, duplicating some of the ports on the back. Front connectors are available for two speaker jacks and for two USB ports. Here we connect the USB ports on the front of the case to two of the available external USB connectors on the motherboard (four are available). I wouldn't guess at these if I didn't have the motherboard documentation because the USB port supplies 5V on one of the leads, which could damage a device or the motherboard if it's connected improperly.

Figure 5.31
Connecting the front panel USB ports

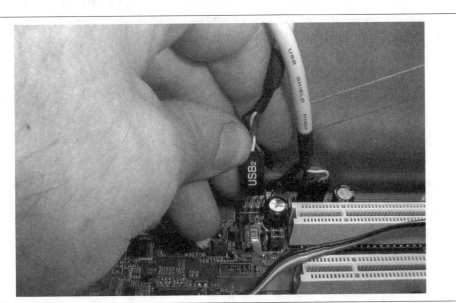

Step 5: Installing the Adapters

I always install the video adapter first, probably in honor of the bad old days when it paid to power up the system as soon as you had a populated motherboard and video just to see if it was working. Six or so years after AGP video was introduced, a locking solution to prevent the adapters popping out of the AGP socket has finally been widely adopted. Before installing the AGP adapter, open the little lock at the front of the slot by pushing it down towards the motherboard.

Figure 5.32
Opening the
AGP slot lock

AGP adapters are keyed to fit only the slots that can support them, with the signal voltage being the overriding consideration. This Crucial Radeon 9800 PRO supports both AGP 4X and 8X with either 1.5V or 0.8V signaling. The motherboard supports 1.5V only, which is why the adapter has more notches than the slot has keys. In order to install the AGP adapter, it's sometimes necessary to start by holding it next to the slot, almost touching the motherboard, and slide the ports out through the slot opening in the back of the case. If the corresponding metal slot blank on the back of the case hasn't been removed yet, lining up the adapter next to the socket will also tell you which one to remove.

Figure 5.33
Crucial Radeon
9800 PRO over
the AGP slot

Once you've slid the ports out the slot opening in the back of the case, you can lift the adapter straight up, and then seat it in the slot, pushing down on the front and back with even force. Depending on the case design, if you don't start by getting the ports out the back of the case, you may find you can't seat the adapter because the metal bracket on the port end keeps hitting the case or the motherboard. Our locking bar system for the adapters still allows us to secure them with screws, but I've seen some locking bar schemes that don't even provide screw holes.

Figure 5.34
Securing the
AGP adapter
with a screw

Like most high-end video adapters, the Crucial Radeon 9800 PRO requires more power than the basic AGP slot design supports. The workaround for this is a direct connection to the ATX power supply, via a drive power connector. The manufacturer suggests a 300-watt minimum power supply be installed for standard configurations, so our 400 watts give a healthy margin of safety.

Figure 5.35
Connecting
power to the
Crucial Radeon
AGP adapter

The final step to installing the AGP adapter is locking it into place. Early AGP adapters were plagued with a design flaw that frequently caused the front of the adapter to lift a little out of the slot over time, because the screw holding down the back of the adapter tended to lever the front end up. Make sure the adapter is fully seated in the slot, then lift the locking latch up and over the projecting tab on the bottom edge of the card. It should go easily, though you can push down on the top of the adapter a little if it's stubborn.

Figure 5.36
Locking the AGP
adapter in place

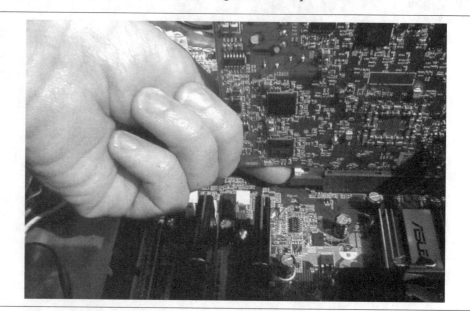

With all of the features on modern motherboards, the AGP adapter may be the only adapter you'll need to install. Since we are going to install two more adapters in our systems, we first want to make sure they won't obstruct any additional motherboard connections in the area. This is the ideal time to attach the audio lead for the DVD recorder so it will be able to play music CDs through the motherboard's integrated music support. In addition to the audio lead for the DVD, shown here, we'll connect the two stereo leads for the front panel connectors, located right next to it.

Figure 5.37
Connecting the audio lead for the DVD recorder

Now as we install our V.92 modem in the PCI slot, you can see it would have been impossible to reach the audio connector with the modem in place. The slot blanks in this case are all punched out of the metal of the case back, just like the I/O shield was, and are removed by bending them back and forth once or twice to fatigue the metal. PCI cards should be handled by the edges and the metal mounting bracket, and then seated with even force applied to the top edge of the adapter.

Figure 5.38
Installing the V.92 modem

Make sure that the ports on the back of the modem are centered in the slot opening before securing it with a screw. If you let the modem lean a little to the side, you'll be able to get the phone jack in, but the spring tab will prevent you from getting it out again until you open the case and remove the modem. That can be very frustrating if you accidentally insert the jack in the phone connector instead of the line connector, resulting in a no dial-tone error.

Figure 5.39
Securing the modem with a screw

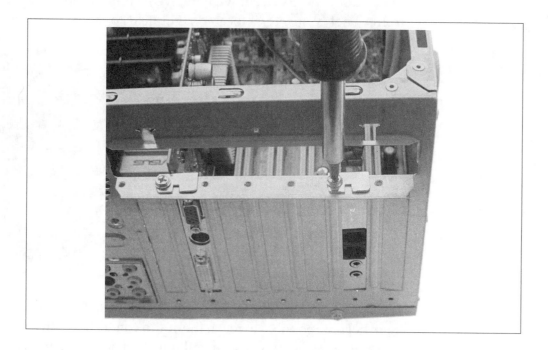

We also installed a PCI wireless adapter, an 802.11b model that's compatible with most older hardware. The wireless adapter is even smaller than the modem, which is why we installed the modem in the second-to-last slot and the wireless adapter to the inside, one slot closer to the video adapter. This arrangement of adapters creates an ample space for airflow from the cooling fan on the AGP adapter. The opening left by our locking bar makes it easy to hold the wireless adapter from the inside and the outside of the case while seating it in the slot.

Figure 5.40
Installing the
wireless adapter

We secure the wireless PCI adapter with a screw. The reason we chose an older standard is that the motherboard ASUS ABV Deluxe motherboard already supports Gigabit Ethernet, and a simple external device is available to enable it for high-speed wireless. When selecting wireless adapters, the main consideration is compatibility with any existing hardware. Older notebooks and home wireless networking solutions are generally based on 802.11b.

Figure 5.41
Securing the
wireless adapter

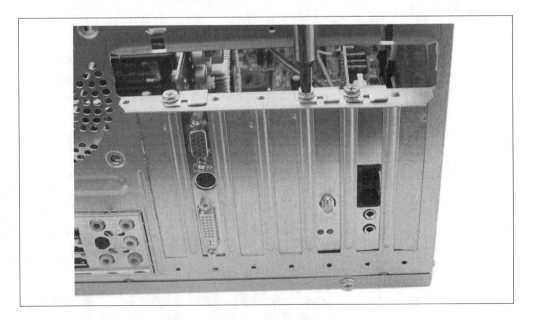

Step 6: Installing the Locking Bar

Now we install the locking bar that's utilized in many recent case designs. There are two T-shaped tabs on the top of the bar, which are being pointed to by the thumbs in this picture. You don't need to do any fancy maneuvering to get the locking bar into place; just fit the projecting tabs into the top of the corresponding slots in the back of the case.

Figure 5.42
Locking bar
with *T* tabs

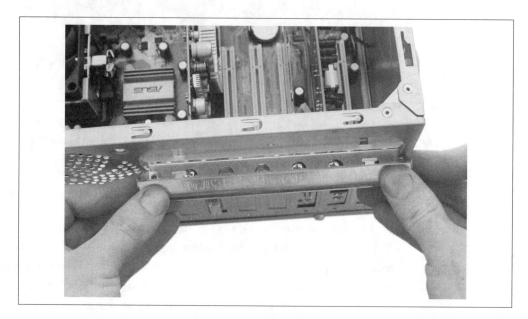

Once the *T* tabs are engaged in the corresponding slots on the back of the case, the locking bar slides straight down onto the adapter brackets. Holes in the locking bar allow the heads of the screws already securing the adapters to project through. There are dimples in the metal of the locking bar tabs that press the adapter brackets to the back of the case, such that the screws probably aren't necessary, but I always use them when possible.

Figure 5.43
Sliding the locking
bar onto the
adapter brackets

The locking bar assembly is secured in place with a single screw in the back of the case. Many cases that employ locking bars don't allow for the adapters to be individually secured by screws, but depending on the design, they often fail to prevent the kind of small lateral movements that can partially obscure a phone jack or adapter port. The adapter-securing method is rarely advertised as a line item in a case description, so if you're buying online and you have a preference, try to find an image of the back of the case before ordering.

Figure 5.44
Securing the
locking bar
with a screw

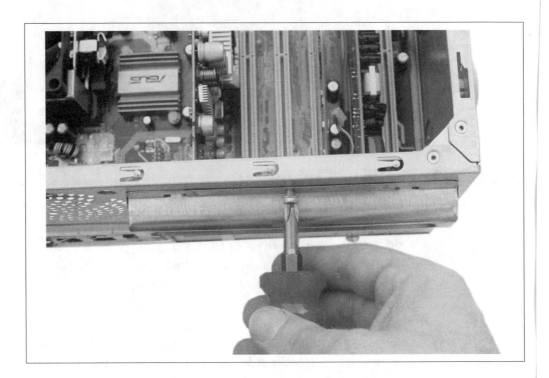

A small antenna is supplied with the wireless adapter and is installed on the connector projecting through the back of the case. It's not particularly critical which way the antenna points, but you don't want it getting in the way or getting broken off. It's traditional to install antennas in an "up" orientation, so we angled this one so it wouldn't project beyond the case edge or interfere with the video monitor connection.

Figure 5.45
Installing the
wireless antenna

Step 7: Installing Drives

Two of the drives we install in this build, the DVD recorder and the floppy
drive, use removable media, which requires that the face of the drive be exposed through the front of the case. Most cases are shipped with a full com-
pliment of blanks installed over the bays, so the first step to install our floppy
drive is to pop out the blank from the top 3.5" drive bay. It's often easier to
get at the blank if you remove the other side panel from the case first, and
you'll have to do this anyway to secure both sides of any installed drives with
screws. The blank is held in from the back, by two plastic locking tabs. Release the tabs from inside the case, and then either pop it out from the back, or
pull it out from the front.

Figure 5.46
Removing a
3.5" bay blank

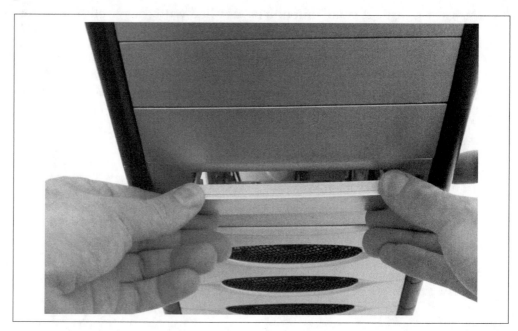

Of all the ribbon connectors used in a PC build, the floppy cable has always been the most problematic to connect. Part of this is due to the open design of the ribbon cable connector on most brands of floppy drives, but the main problem is that the small format drives are often difficult to access or see clearly once they are installed in the case. The remedy for this is to connect the floppy ribbon cable to the drive before installing the drive in the case.

Figure 5.47
Connecting the floppy ribbon cable

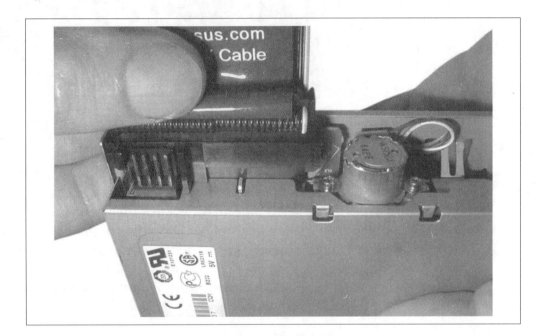

Once the ribbon cable is connected to the floppy drive, feed the cable in through the opening in the front facade, and slide the drive in after it, making sure it is upside up (the label is on the top). There are usually a couple metal tabs or guides punched out of the walls of the 3.5" bays that will support the drive as you slide it in. If the drive feels like it wants to drop into the case, either the tabs aren't present and you'll have to level the drive by eye, or you're dropping it below the back guides.

Figure 5.48
Installing the
floppy drive

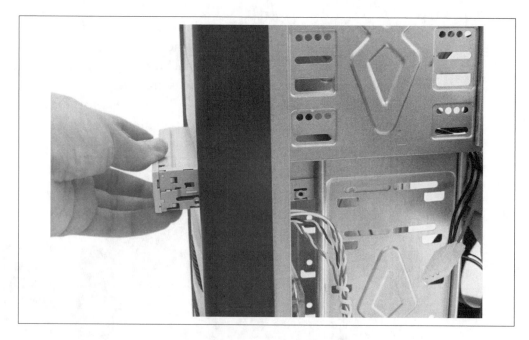

Make sure the faceplate of the drive is flush with the front facade, secure it with one screw, and then double-check the alignment from the front. While it's not really necessary to secure the floppy drive with all four screws, it doesn't hurt. Also, it ensures you'll have an available supply of fine-thread screws right in the case if you ever find you're short a couple when installing additional drives later on.

Figure 5.49
Securing the
floppy drive

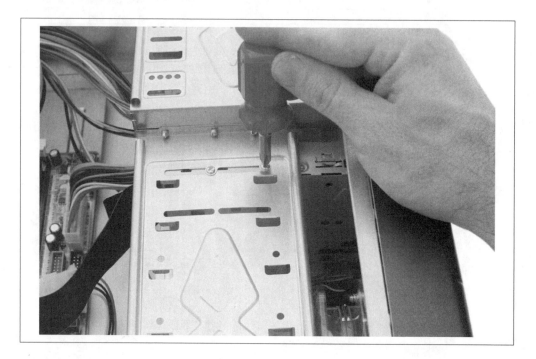

The next step to installing our floppy drive is to connect the other end of the ribbon cable to the floppy controller on the motherboard. This ASUS motherboard mounts the floppy connector on the edge of the motherboard, and it's actually easier to make the connection from the back of the motherboard than from the front. Since the cable is supplied with the motherboard, the connector is keyed to fit only in the proper orientation.

Figure 5.50
Connecting the ribbon cable to the floppy controller

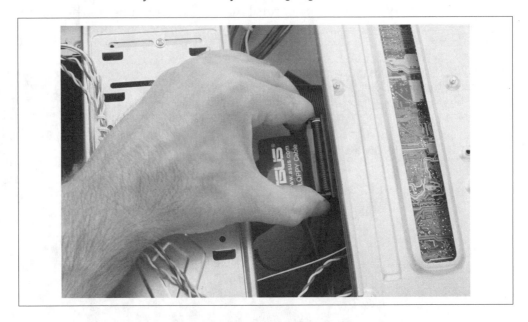

The last step to installing the floppy drive is to connect the small-format power connector. Unlike the other power connectors in the system, the small-format connectors can sometimes be forced on upside down by accident. The flat side of the connector is the bottom, and should snug up against a tab under the four power pins.

Figure 5.51
Connecting power to the floppy drive

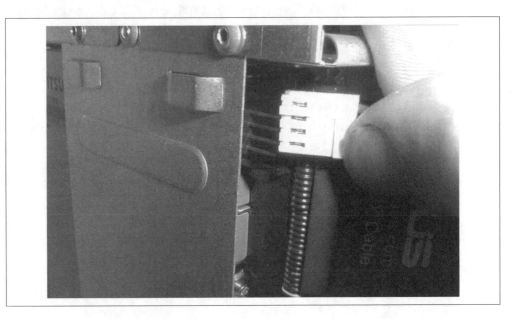

We began the hard drive installation in this case by connecting the SATA cable to the motherboard, because installing the hard drive first would have made it difficult to get a clean picture of the connectors. See our Pentium 4 build in Chapter 6 for connecting older IDE hard drives with parallel IDE interfaces. The cable is keyed with a hole on one end, so it can't be put on backwards. There's no latching mechanism on the motherboard, so you have to be careful not to pull the cable off the connection when you're working in the case.

Figure 5.52
Connecting the SATA cable to the motherboard

Next we install the hard drive in the case, upside up, though most hard drives are designed to operate when mounted sideways or upside down as well. Since we installed the motherboard first, it was a little tricky in this tight case to maneuver the hard drive into place without banging into the motherboard. You can't put the drive in the bay on any angle, and then turn it up, because the corner-to-corner dimension is greater than the side-to-side measurement. However, the lower 3.5" bays usually don't have the wall guides present in the upper bays, so you can start with the drive in the bottom bay and slide it up.

Figure 5.53
Installing the
80 GB SATA
hard drive

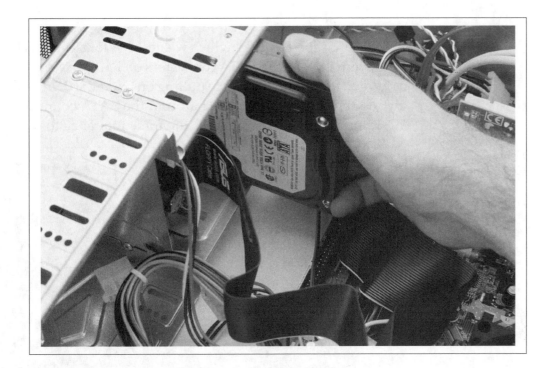

Secure the hard drive with four coarse thread screws, two from each side of the case. It's more important to get four screws into the drive and for the drive to be mounted level than to mount the drive as close as possible to the front facade. I also like to leave a little extra space between drives for air circulation whenever possible, which is why the drive is mounted in a lower bay, rather than right under the floppy.

Figure 5.54
Securing the
hard drive

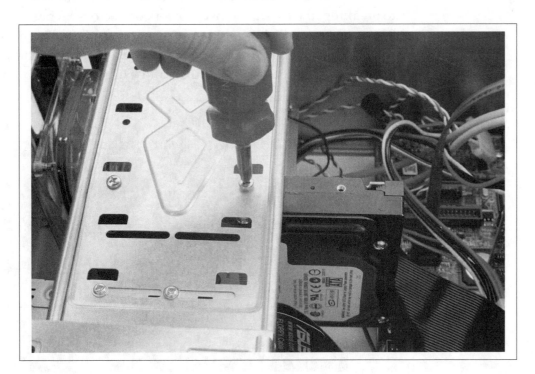

Our Western Digital hard drive supports their proprietary SecureConnect ATA cable, which we decided to use in this build. According to Western Digital, the SATA connectors on hard drives can be broken off by as little as four pounds of force pulling on a standard SATA cable. The plastic guides and reinforced housing around the SATA connectors on supported Western Digital drives increases the force tolerance to over 20 pounds.

Figure 5.55
Connecting the SATA secure cable connection

The downside of using the SecureConnect cable is that it only handles the SATA data. This means we still need to use a legacy power connector for the drive, rather than the small-format SATA power connector. While not prone to breaking, the old-fashioned power connectors on hard drives take a bit of force to insert, which is another reason to use all four screws in securing the drive. The connector doesn't need to seat all the way to the stop ridge, just as long as it goes in a good half inch and can't be easily pulled out.

Figure 5.56
Connecting hard drive power

The final drive we install is our Dual Layer DVD recorder. The blank for the 5.25" bay is popped out from behind, just like the blank for the floppy bay. The drive slides in from the front and is supported by the projecting tabs from the bay wall. For an example of a 5.25" drive in a case that requires premounted rails, see our Pentium 4 build in Chapter 6. If the drive feels like it's sagging into the case, stop and make sure that the bay has supporting metal tabs. If it doesn't, lay the case on its side before installing the drive so it doesn't drop.

Figure 5.57
Sliding the
DVD recorder
into the case

Make sure that the faceplate of the drive is aligned with the front of the case and secure it with four fine-thread screws, two from each side. If the drive shipped with a small plastic bag of special screws, use those, because they may be shorter than the standard fine-thread screws to prevent interference with the tray mechanism.

Figure 5.58
Securing the
DVD recorder

Next we connect the audio lead that allows the DVD drive to play music CDs through the computer's sound system. The other end of the lead was connected in Figure 5-37, before we populated the surrounding area with PCI adapters. The four-wire connector has a small latch on the top, so once you connect it, it won't pull out without that latch being depressed.

Figure 5.59
Installing the audio lead for playing music CDs

Next we install the IDE ribbon cable that carries the data. One of the cables that was shipped with our ASUS motherboard is labeled CD-ROM, meaning that it's a standard 40-wire IDE cable not suited for high-transfer rate IDE hard drives. So far, the transfer rates of even the fastest DVD players are low enough that they don't require the 80-wire ribbon cable used for modern IDE hard drives.

Figure 5.60
Connecting the DVD data cable

The power connection to the DVD drive utilizes a standard, large-format connector from the power supply. We reserved one of the cable bundles from the power supply for connections at the top of the case, and used the other cable for the lower connections. Due to the number of auxiliary connections made in this build, including two case fans and the power boost for the AGP video card, it took a little planning ahead to end up being able to reach all the devices without having to start rearranging all the connections when something doesn't reach.

Figure 5.61
Connecting power to the DVD recorder

The last step to install our DVD recorder is to connect the other end of the ribbon cable to the IDE controller on the motherboard. Even though we aren't using any parallel IDE hard drives in this system, we connected the IDE cable to the secondary controller out of habit. If the drives get changed out in the future, it may help avoid confusion. Like all of the ribbon cables supplied with the ASUS motherboard, the connection is keyed with blocks in the cable header so it can only be connected in the proper orientation.

Figure 5.62
Connecting the
IDE cable to the
controller

Step 8: Final Details Before Closing the Case

AMD recommends an additional exhaust fan be installed when using an
Athlon 64. Since this is a fairly cramped case, we saved mounting the additional fan for one of the last steps so it wouldn't create another obstruction
when we fit and installed the motherboard. The fan is installed with the label
toward the grille, because the airflow is in the direction of the label.

Figure 5.63
Installing an
additional
exhaust fan

There are available locations for two additional exhaust fans on this case, with predrilled holes. If your fan isn't sold with mounting hardware, simply use some short, thick wood screws that will tap their own thread into the plastic frame of the fan and hold it securely. The fan uses an inline power connection just like the intake fan connection shown in Figure 5-29.

Figure 5.64
Securing the
exhaust fan on
the case back

The hotter the components in the case (in terms of both heat and performance), the more you have to worry about maintaining good airflow through the case. The intake fan at the bottom of the front facade, the additional exhaust fan, and the series exhaust fan on the power supply can certainly move the air through, but it's a good idea to minimize the tangle of cables that break up the airflow in the case. A few standard cable ties work well to bundle the cables together; just don't put them on too tight or you'll have trouble cutting them off without damaging the cables if you ever need to make a change. Trim off the excess tie with scissors or wire cutters.

Figure 5.65
Bundling cables
with a tie

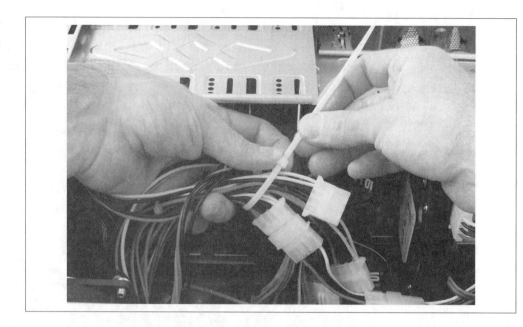

Finally, double-check all of your connections before putting the down side panel (the one under the motherboard) back on the case. Make sure that you haven't left any heavy tools, like a screwdriver or pliers, anywhere in or on the case, and then lift the case with both hands with the motherboard level, and slowly tilt it back and forth. If you hear anything rolling around, take the down side panel back off and make sure a screw or standoff actually falls out. Reinstall the panel and repeat the tilting process. Never connect the power to a PC if you heard a screw rolling around inside and couldn't find it. It could be that there's a screw stuck between the bottom of the motherboard and the case infrastructure, waiting to cause a short circuit as soon as you connect the power.

Figure 5.66
Final inspection
before closing
the case

Replace the top side panel, check that the voltage switch on the back of the power supply is set to the proper voltage for your country, and connect the power cord. See our Pentium 4 build in Chapter 6 for checking the voltage selector, and see the end of Chapter 3 for connecting peripherals.

Step 9: Initial CMOS Settings

We enter CMOS Setup the first time we power up the system by tapping the DEL repeatedly. The main screen shows that our NEC DVD recorder is recognized on the secondary IDE master, but note that it doesn't even have a line item for registering the SATA drives. The SATA settings are controlled through a dedicated SATA BIOS that can also be accessed by pressing the TAB key at the appropriate time during boot.

Figure 5.67
Standard CMOS Settings

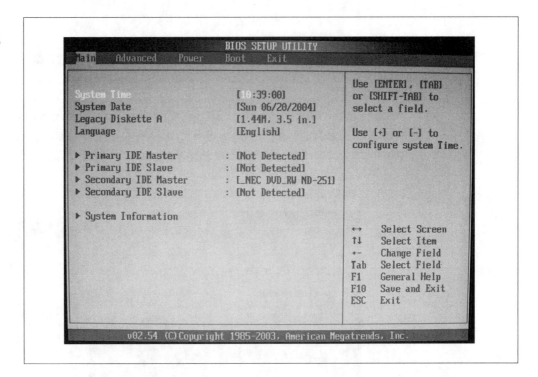

Following the instructions that came with the motherboard, we immediately go into the advanced menu, select CPU Configuration, and bring up the Memory Configuration screen. The ASUS instructions detailed a number of changes to be made in the basic memory parameters, but there's no point in listing them here because they will almost certainly be different for whatever system you build. The point is to follow the instructions for CMOS Setup that accompany the motherboard.

Figure 5.68
Memory
Configuration

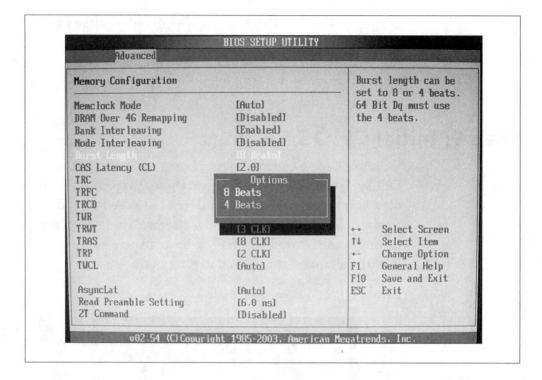

Next we enter the AGP Bridge Configuration submenu to make sure the AGP speed has been properly identified as 8X and to set the graphics aperture (in accordance with the ASUS instructions) to 256 MB.

Figure 5.69
AGP Configuration

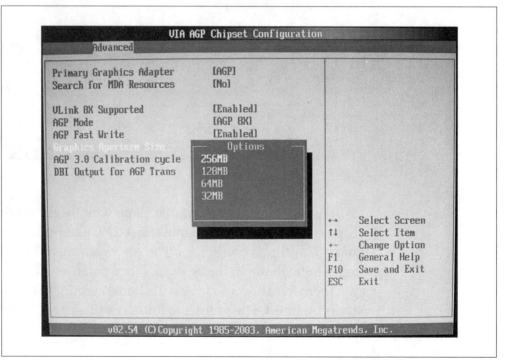

The next menu will be of interest to overclockers, although with a Athlon 64 3800+, I was quite happy to settle for the standard settings. The ASUS motherboard supports adaptive overclocking, along with some standard increments, and manual overclocking. In the manual mode, you can select the FSB and CPU frequency, plus voltage boosts for the CPU core, the DDR memory, and even the AGP adapter.

Figure 5.70
AI Overclocking

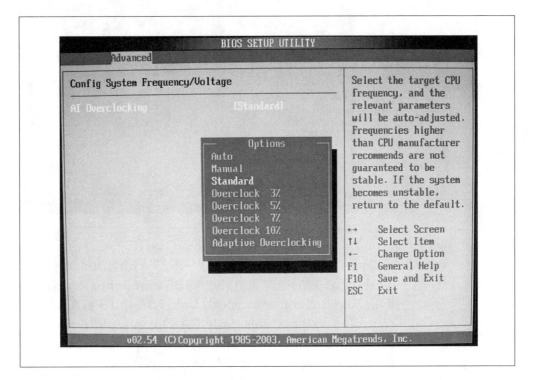

The final CMOS Setup screen we'll look at is the Hardware Monitor screen under the Power tab. It's important to make sure that your new CPU isn't going into thermal runaway even while idling by watching the screen for a few minutes until the CPU temperature stabilizes. You can keep an eye on the power supply output at the same time. It's normal for the voltage readings, which are measured in discrete units larger than the decimal accuracy of the readout, to flip back and forth between two values. If the voltage rises and falls through a large range of different values and doesn't stabilize with time, you have a problem power supply.

Figure 5.71
Hardware Monitor

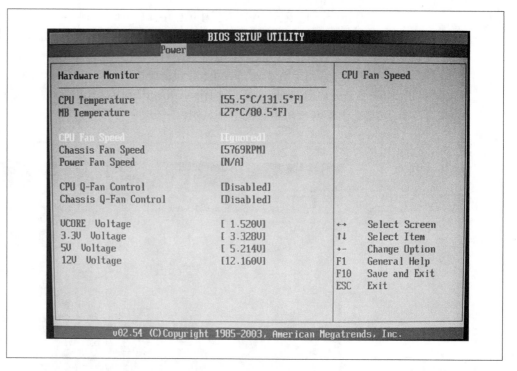

Finally, we'll pop into the VIA SATA BIOS for correct identification of our hard drive. Even though the ASUS motherboard sports a Promise FastTrak RAID controller that supports both IDE and SATA RAIDs, the standard ATA controller also features basic RAID configurations. With just one drive installed, we won't be creating a RAID, but see our builds in Chapters 4 and 6 for connecting drives to RAID controllers.

Figure 5.72
VIA Chipset
SATA BIOS screen

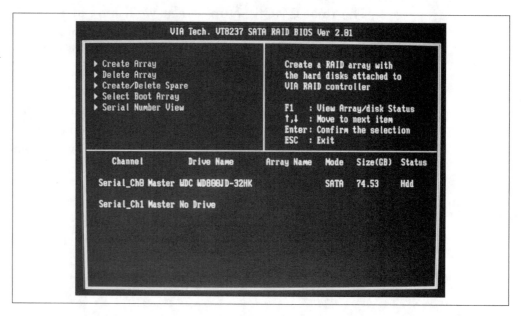

Chapter 6

Building a Pentium 4 in a Tower Case

Step 1: Preparing the Case

We chose to build our Pentium 4 in a tower case to better illustrate the IDE RAID and SCSI disk subsystems we include as options. Tower cases tend to be top heavy, so they are often constructed with fold-out feet on the bottom for stability. This tower case features a drive access door that can be locked, a handy feature for a classroom server.

Figure 6.1
Tower case

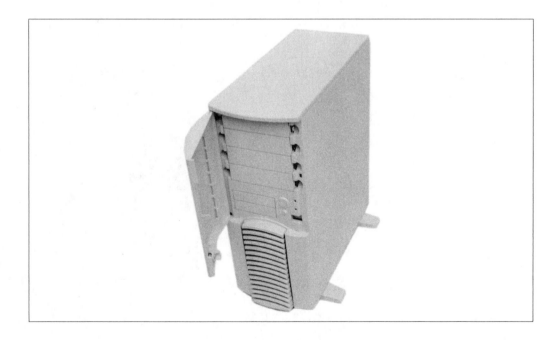

There are two basic varieties of tower and midtower case designs. The sides, or lids, of this tower are secured with two screws at the back of the case and the front facade is never removed. The other approach is to hide all the screws under the front facade. To open the case, we begin by removing the screws from the top lid, which is the left side of any tower or midtower PC.

Figure 6.2
Removing the screw securing the case lid

Another feature of this tower case is the lockable release handle on the lid. Even after the screws are taken out, if the release handle is locked, the lid can't be removed. Security features are common on tower cases, which tend to be loaded with expensive components and "easy out" designs for mounting the drives. The release is pushed in and the lid is lifted away from the case.

Figure 6.3
Releasing the lid

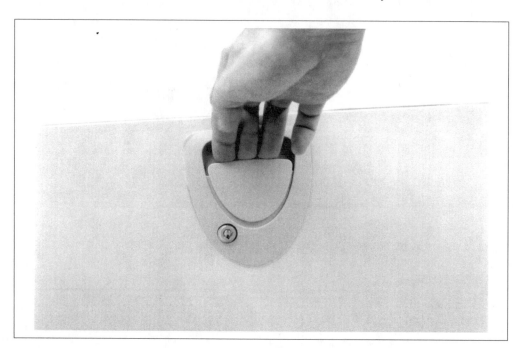

One of the benefits of buying an upscale case is the engineering design. The tower came stock with two exhaust fans (bottom left) and provides snap-in installation for up to two intake fans at the front. The 5.25" drive bays all employ rails, which are stored in holders on the bottom of the case. The screws and other hardware are taped in place between the rail holders.

Figure 6.4
Tower case features

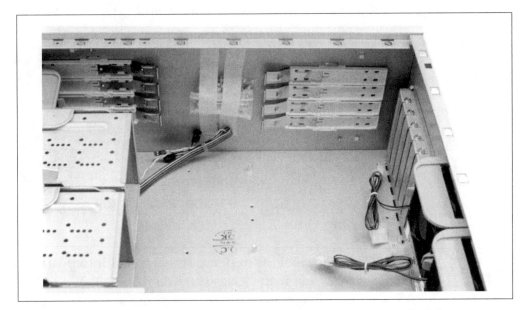

The Intel D850MD motherboard we are installing is shipped with its own I/O shield. The standard I/O shield with which all cases ship is equipped with punch-outs that will match the majority of motherboard I/O cores, but the five USB ports in our motherboard I/O core exceed the standard design. The first step is to remove the stock I/O shield by pushing it into the case. You might need to pry with a flat-bladed screwdriver to get it started.

Figure 6.5
Popping out the stock I/O core shield

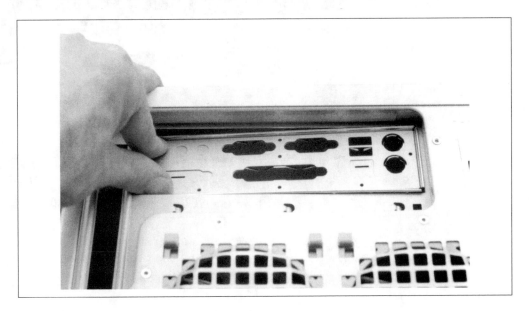

The new I/O shield is installed from the inside of the case. The smooth side of the I/O shield, which is stamped with symbols describing port functions, faces out through the opening. The inward side of the I/O shield is identified by the springy metal tabs for grounding the ports to the case. The two circular holes, one above the other, are the keyboard and mouse ports, and the shield is installed so these end up closest to the power supply.

Figure 6.6
Positioning the
new I/O shield

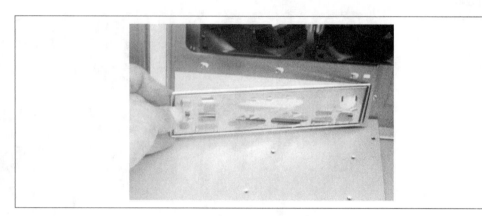

Once the shield is in place, it's snapped into position by pushing at the edges from inside the case. The shield is designed with the edges doubled over and projecting outward, providing a natural spring effect to hold the shield in place. In some cases the standard I/O opening is a little oversized so the shield doesn't want to stay in place, but once the motherboard is installed it will be locked in.

Figure 6.7
New I/O shield
snapped into
place from inside
the case

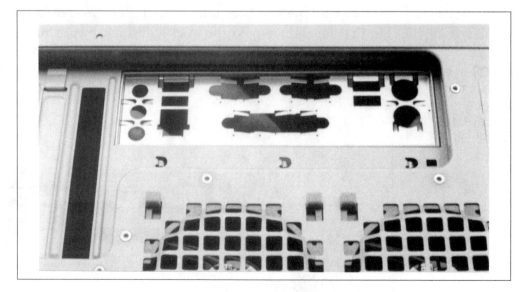

We purchased one additional case fan, commonly called a *muffin fan*, to draw air into the case through the front facade vents. Muffin fans draw air in the direction of the label on the motor, and this fan will complement the two exhaust fans on the back of the tower. When adding fans to a case, it's important to establish an airflow direction, usually front to back, and make sure all fans move the air in the same direction, rather than fighting each other.

Figure 6.8
Muffin fan

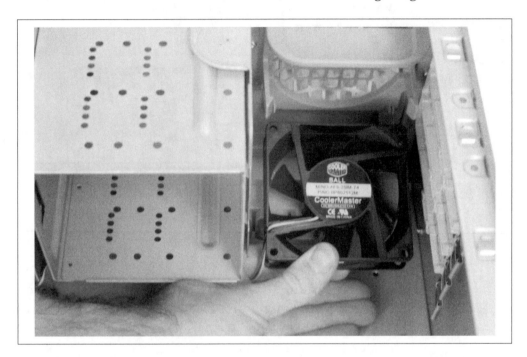

The fan is installed in this case simply by snapping it into place. The through holes in the four corners of the muffin fan align with pegs in the holder, and the two plastic retainers snap over the fan body. This is a tremendous improvement over cases that require you to mount any additional fans with four slender bolts or long plastic rivets. The bolts or rivets are rarely supplied with either the case or the fan, which forces you to run out to a hardware store to continue.

Figure 6.9
Snapping the
muffin fan
in place

Step 2: Installing CPU and Heatsink

The motherboard in this build is the first to support the Pentium 4 in Socket 478. It features dual-channel RDRAM support, integrated audio, 10/100 BaseT networking, and five USB ports. The micro ATX layout only supports three PCI expansion slots (the vertical white slots to the bottom right), but with the integrated features and all those USB ports, that's more than enough for most applications.

Figure 6.10
Intel D850MD
motherboard

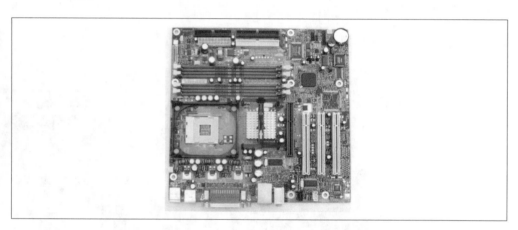

The Pentium 4 for Socket 478 is physically smaller than the original Pentium 4, due largely to the smaller dimensions employed on the silicon level. The chip is keyed to the socket with a missing pin in one corner, so it can't be inserted the wrong way.

Figure 6.11
Pentium 4 keyed
to Socket 478

The first step to installing the CPU is to lift the locking lever on the side of the socket. Move the lever a little away from the side of the socket to free it from the hold-down, and gently pull it up until it stops. It shouldn't require any force to move the locking lever. You can actually lift it with one finger once it's past the hold-down.

Figure 6.12
Lifting the
locking lever

The Pentium 4 is placed in the socket with the keyed corner, also marked by the black dot, matching the socket key. The locking lever is lowered back into the tuck position. Don't be surprised by the great change in resistance between raising the lever and lowering it. The lever locks 478 pins in place by spring force.

Figure 6.13
Locking the
Pentium 4
in place

The Pentium 4 heatsink for Socket 478 actually consists of three pieces. The first of these, the retention module, came permanently mounted on the motherboard. The two pieces shown here are the retention clip and the active heatsink, a fan mounted on a finned aluminum structure that maximizes surface area to disperse the heat.

Figure 6.14
Active heatsink
and retention clip

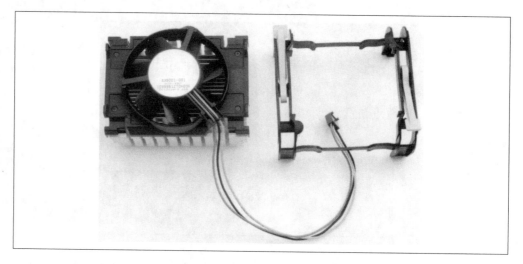

The dark area on the bottom of the heatsink is a pre-applied thermal interface, saving us from the need to apply thermal grease to the CPU package. The retention clip is placed over the heatsink, and the whole assembly is lowered into the retention module. The heatsink settles over the CPU, held a slight distance above it by the pads in the corners of the retention module.

Figure 6.15
Lowering the
heatsink and
retention clip
into place

The retention clip fits loosely over the heatsink, with four clips lined up with the four holes in the retention module posts. Push the whole retention mechanism down over the heatsink to lock the individual clips in place. These clips make an audible "click" as they are pushed over the retention module, but the whole assembly sits quite loosely.

Figure 6.16
Seating the retention clip over the heatsink and retention module

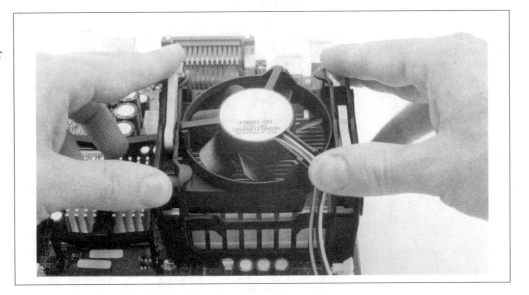

The two levers that force the heatsink into contact with the CPU and lock the whole assembly into place actually move in opposite directions. Lift both levers (I do this simultaneously) and bring them all the way over until they lock down in the opposite positions. This takes even more force than the locking lever on the CPU socket.

Figure 6.17
Locking the heatsink assembly into place

As soon as the active heatsink is locked in place, attach the fan to the CPU fan point on the motherboard, normally labeled "fan 1." This allows the motherboard BIOS (Basic I/O System) to monitor the CPU fan speed and manage it in power saver and sleep modes. In this instance, the fan 1 connector was the closest connector to the CPU socket, but this isn't always the case, so check the motherboard documentation.

Figure 6.18
Connecting
the CPU fan

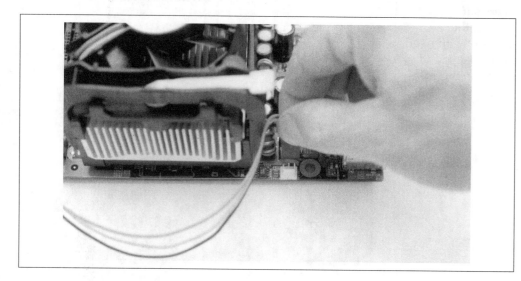

Step 3: Installing Memory

The D850MD motherboard supports two banks of RDRAM, for a total of up to 2 GB of memory. We are installing two pieces of 128 MB RDRAM, for a total of 256 MB. The RIMM modules are keyed with two notches so they can't be installed backward. The positions of the notches on these Kingston modules are marked by circular indents with black dots on the bottom of the metal module cover.

Figure 6.19
128 MB Kingston
RIMM over
RDRAM socket

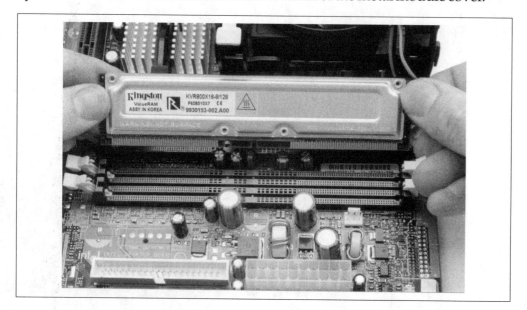

Before installing any modules, make sure the white locking levers on the sides of the sockets are spread. As you seat the module by applying even pressure with two thumbs, the white levers will raise into position. This requires a good deal of pressure, so do this with the motherboard placed on its static bag on a hard, flat surface.

Figure 6.20
Seating the
first RIMM

The second RIMM is installed in the same bank as the first, filling Bank 0 before Bank 1. RIMM modules are only 8 bits wide, so it takes two modules to make up the 16-bit dual-channel memory bus width. The metal covers of the RIMMs carry a warning to not touch them when the computer has been running, because they get very hot.

Figure 6.21
Seating the
second RIMM

The RDRAM architecture requires that all empty sockets be filled with CRIMMs, empty circuit boards that provide continuity to the bus. The CRIMMs are aligned with two notches, the same as the RIMMs. Make sure the locking levers are spread, and seat the CRIMMs with even pressure from two thumbs. If you prefer to install your memory modules with the motherboard in the case, make sure there is sufficient support under the memory socket area to bear the load of the insertion force.

Figure 6.22
CRIMM over socket

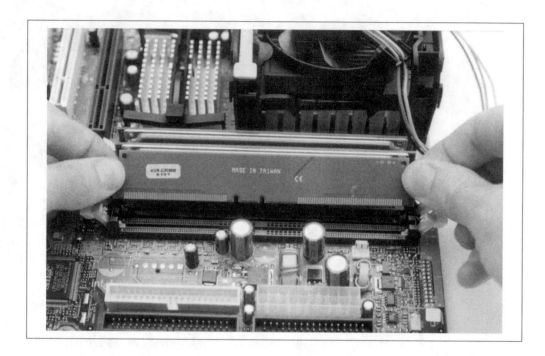

Our two RIMMs are installed in Bank 0 and our two CRIMMs are installed in Bank 1. This motherboard is entirely jumperless, meaning that the CPU and memory configuration is automatic. In all instances, check the motherboard manual for any settings, and make sure the defaults are actually selected on your motherboard.

Figure 6.23
Completed
memory
installation

Step 4: Installing the Motherboard

The next step is to test-fit the motherboard in the case. Use two hands to hold the motherboard over any existing standoffs and to check the fit with the I/O shield. Next, count the number of silver rimmed holes in the motherboard that line up with holes in the case (all of them should). Set the motherboard off to the side on its static bag and remove any standoffs that don't line up with the holes in your board.

Figure 6.24
Test-fitting the
motherboard

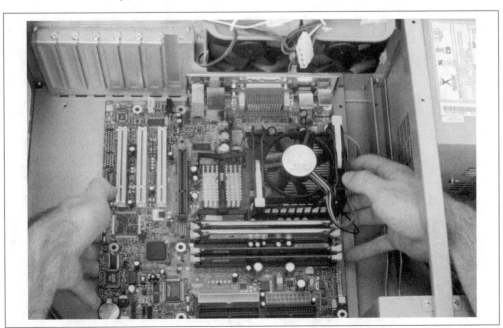

Install standoffs in the case holes that match your motherboard. Do not use standoffs that ship with the motherboard unless you remove all the standoffs that are installed in the case. Slight differences in standoff height can put unacceptable stress on the motherboard. The standoffs that shipped with this case are the standard brass type, which can be tightened with a nutdriver or pliers, but don't overtighten or they may break.

Figure 6.25
Installing a
brass standoff

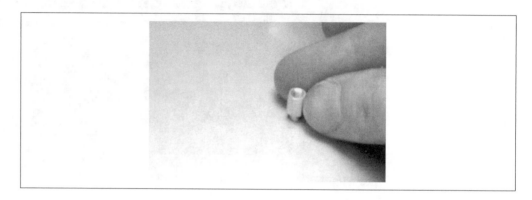

Count the number of standoffs installed and set aside that number of screws. Reinstall the motherboard in the case, securing the corners first. It's usually best to start with the corner by the memory sockets, across from the I/O core. The little tabs on the I/O shield can apply enough spring force that you need to really keep the motherboard pushed into the shield as you install the screw. Secure the other corners, then fill in the other screws. If you finish with one of your set-aside screws left over, remove the motherboard and take out the standoff that didn't line up with a hole.

Figure 6.26
Installing a
motherboard screw

Here you can see the I/O core of the installed motherboard properly aligned with the I/O shield. Above the I/O core are the two exhaust fans. The airflow direction can be confirmed by noting that the labels on the fan motors are visible through the grate.

Figure 6.27
I/O core aligned with I/O shield

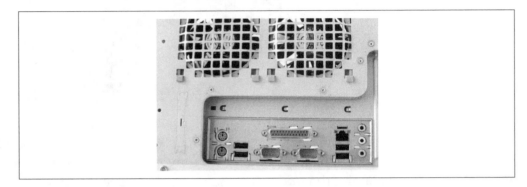

The next step is to attach the main ATX power connector to the motherboard. The 20-wire connector is keyed so that it can only be installed one way, and is automatically secured by the plastic spring latch. The power supply should not be plugged in or switched on until the build is complete.

Figure 6.28
Attaching the ATX power connector

With the introduction of the Pentium 4, Intel required an additional 12V lead from the power supply to the motherboard. Some P4 motherboards use an old-fashioned AT power connector to supply additional power for the CPU or AGP Pro slot, but none of our builds uses one of these. The P4 might run without the additional 12V lead, but it isn't recommended.

Figure 6.29
Attaching the
12V header

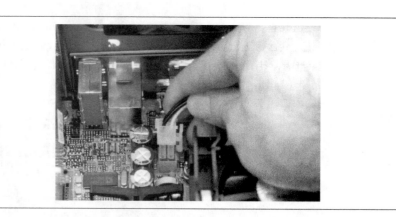

The muffin fan that we previously installed in the front of the case needs a power connection, and one is conveniently located nearby on the corner of the motherboard. Using the motherboard connection means the computer can monitor the fan status. If additional muffin fans were employed, they would be powered directly from power supply leads.

Figure 6.30
Attaching the
muffin fan
power lead

The most important of the front panel leads to the motherboard is the power switch. This two-wire connector can go on the proper two posts either way, unlike LEDs, which will only work with the correct polarity. The circular unit below and slightly to the left of the connection block is an onboard piezoelectric speaker, eliminating the need for a case speaker connection.

Figure 6.31
Attaching the
power lead to the
motherboard

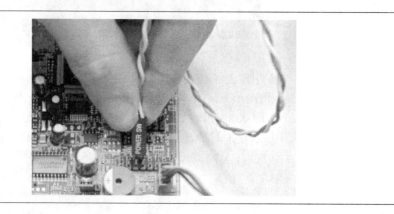

Step 5: Installing Adapters

We install our 4X video adapter with 32 MB of video memory in the single AGP slot. This 3D AGP Phantom was a premier gaming card just a couple years ago, but it's been surpassed by new graphics accelerators with eight times the memory and double the bus speed. You must install the factory video driver after you install the operating system to fully utilize the capabilities of the video adapter.

Figure 6.32
Installing the
AGP adapter

Secure the adapter with a screw on the back rail immediately after installation. Make sure the front edge of the adapter doesn't come out of the AGP slot as the back edge is forced down by the screw. Note that the PCI slot next to any video adapter with a heatsink on the video processor is nearly useless. Even though you can fit an adapter in, it will be too close to the heatsink to allow for decent air circulation.

Figure 6.33
Securing the
AGP adapter

Planning and foresight can save you a lot of wasted steps when you build a PC. We know we will be installing a DVD at a later point, and we know that the motherboard has integrated sound. For the DVD to play music CDs, the stereo lead must be connected to the proper point on the sound card or, in this case, motherboard. Because that point happens to be between the PCI slots, we take the time to do it right now.

Figure 6.34
Attaching the stereo lead for the DVD

The 56 Kb/s modem is installed in the second PCI slot, a safe distance from the heatsink on the video card. For our basic build, these are the only two adapters we need to install, because all the other features we want are integrated on the motherboard. The adapter is jumperless and all of the settings are handled from within Windows.

Figure 6.35
Installing the modem

There are two tricks to installing any adapter with recessed ports. The first trick is to make sure the ports actually line up with the slot in the back of the case, so that the connectors, telephone jacks in this case, can be inserted and removed. The second trick is getting the screw into the adapter when the rail is recessed under the edge of the case. All of the pictures in this book show the screw being tightened by a screwdriver, but I usually start them by hand.

Figure 6.36
Starting
the modem
hold-down screw

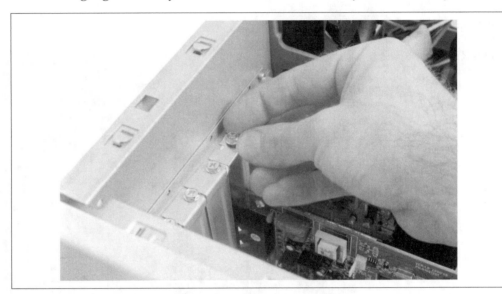

Step 6: Installing the Drives

The reason for choosing this tower case is the elegant construction of the drive cages. Because we will be illustrating IDE RAID and SCSI options on this system in later steps, we'll be replacing and removing many hard drives. The first step is usually to install the floppy drive and boot hard drive in the top cage. The cage is secured by a simple locking lever, pulled back here by the thumb.

Figure 6.37
Removing the
drive cage

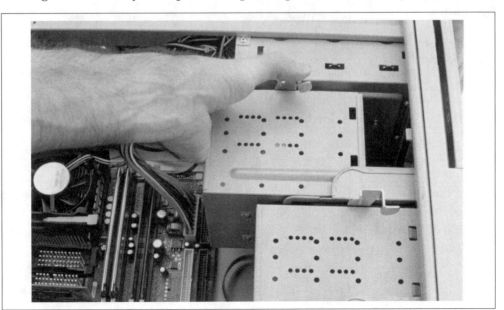

There are so many possible mounting locations for the floppy drive in this cage that we need to do a test fitting. The first step is to remove the metal RF shield blocking the floppy port. These are held in place by metal tabs, which are broken by wiggling the shield back and forth. In some instances you may have to remove both shields to get the floppy drive aligned with the opening in the front facade.

Figure 6.38
Removing the metal RF shield

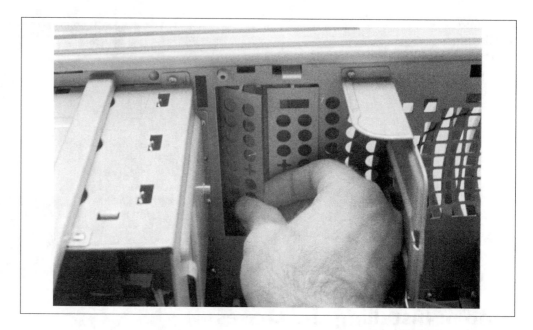

The white plastic blank on the front facade blocking the opening is popped out from behind with the fingers. Now you can replace the cage in its position and lock it in place. Slide the floppy drive in from the front until the faceplate is flush with the facade, then insert a single screw to hold it in that position.

Figure 6.39
Finding the correct floppy drive position

Remove the cage and secure the floppy drive with three more fine-thread screws. Some PC builders have abandoned floppy drives altogether, because most software is delivered on CD or over the Internet. Floppy drives do have many problems, as we detailed in the introductory chapters, but for the extra $10, it's worth installing one.

Figure 6.40
Securing the
floppy with
four fine-thread
screws

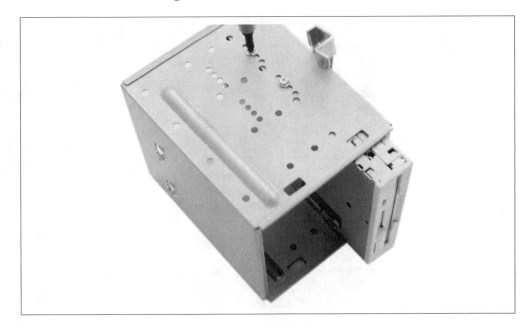

Next we install the hard drive in the bottom of the cage. The 80 GB Maxtor drive could have been installed in the middle of the cage, but it's always a good idea to put as much space as possible between drives. The connectors must face into the case, and I always install hard drives so they will run upside up, even though the manufacturers claim they are just as happy upside down.

Figure 6.41
Securing the hard
drive with four
coarse screws

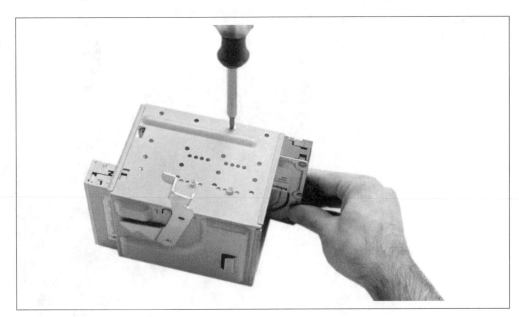

The cage is slid back into the case with the drives installed. Even though we lined up the floppy drive with the opening, it might take some jiggling to get it in, and we may have to remove the metal RF shield for the other 3.5" opening. As soon as the cage is installed, lock it into place with the lever. Otherwise, it can come sliding out when you stand up the case and crash into the motherboard.

Figure 6.42
Installing the
loaded drive cage

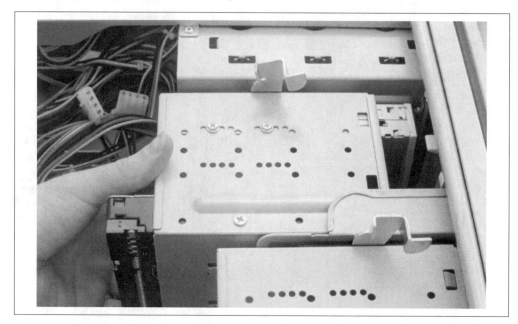

The 5.25" drives in this tower are rail mounted. Proper rail position is determined by experimentation, but they normally mount as far forward as they can go, with the rail positioned as close to the bottom of the drive as possible. Even when doing a trial fit, attach both rails with two fine-thread screws each, and if you guess right, you're done.

Figure 6.43
Installing rails on
the DVD drive

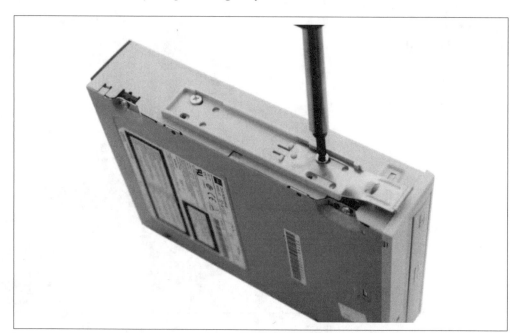

Pop the plastic bay cover out from inside the case in the bay without the RF shield. Case manufacturers assume that every PC will be built with at least a 5.25" drive, so one bay is left unshielded. Slide the drive slowly into the case, stopping if it binds. A common mistake is to position the rails differently on the two sides of the drive. When the drive settles in place, you shouldn't be able to push it out from the back without depressing the spring clips from the front.

Figure 6.44
Installing the DVD drive

Step 7: Connecting the Drives

There is no rule for the order in which drive connections should be made, as long as they are made correctly. We begin here with the floppy ribbon cable connection to the motherboard. The connector is usually keyed, but you should still double-check that the red key wire in the cable is oriented to the pin 1 end of the connector, often marked with an arrow.

Figure 6.45
Connecting the floppy ribbon cable to the motherboard

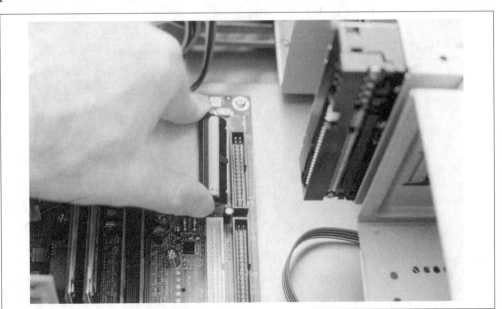

The connector on the other end of the ribbon cable is connected to the back of the floppy drive, with the red key wire again toward pin 1 on the drive. This ribbon cable connection is probably the most problematic connection in building a PC. The cable can be forced on missing an entire row of pins, as detailed in Chapter 3.

Figure 6.46
Installing the floppy ribbon cable

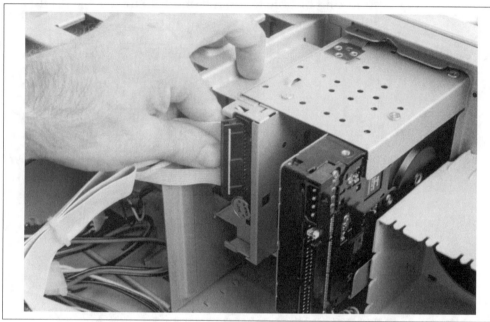

The small format power connector also causes more problems than any other power connector in the system. There is a rectangular indent on one side of the connector that matches a rectangular tab under the four pins on the drive. The protruding ridge visible on the side of the connector shown here should prevent the connector from being installed upside down, but it pays to take a good look at the drive if it doesn't fit on easily.

Figure 6.47
Connecting power to the floppy drive

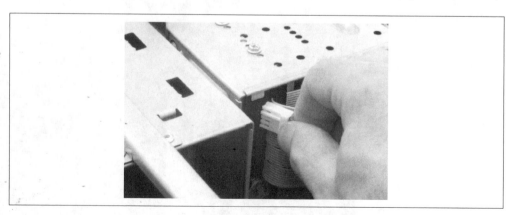

Connect the blue header on the 80-conductor ribbon cable to the primary IDE controller on the motherboard. The connection is keyed to fit one way only. One of the advantages of buying a hard drive in a retail pack is you are sure to get a quality 80-conductor ribbon cable. When you see that the hard drive is close to the motherboard connection, you can fold up the slack in the cable and catch it with a cable clamp, tie-wrap, or, failing all else, a thin rubber band.

Figure 6.48
Attaching the ribbon cable to the primary IDE controller

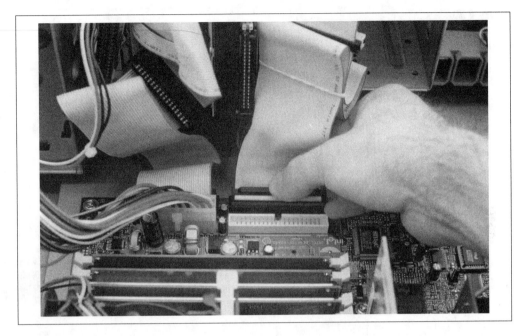

The master drive on a high-speed IDE controller (ATA133, ATA100 or ATA66) must be attached to the far end of the 80-conductor ribbon cable, using the black connector. The connection is keyed to work one way only, but you can double-check that the red key wire is toward the power connector. The cable will perform the Master/Slave selection.

Figure 6.49
Connecting the ribbon cable to the hard drive

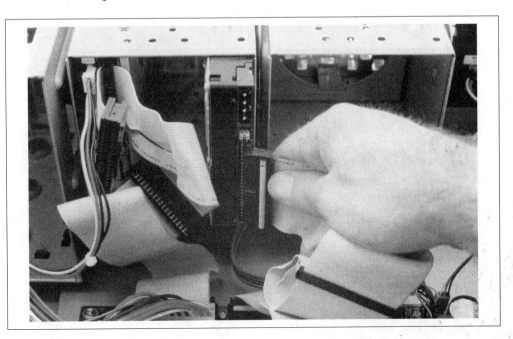

The large format connector used for hard drives and CD/DVDs can only be inserted one way, thanks to two angle-cut corners. The connector might not push in all the way to the ridge stop, but it should go in far enough that it doesn't pull out easily.

Figure 6.50
Connecting power to the hard drive

The most overlooked connection in PC assembly is the stereo lead from the CD/DVD, without which you can't play music CDs in your PC. This has nothing to do with the sound used in PC games or the operating system, so a PC is often in use for a long time before somebody tries to play a CD and realizes something is wrong. The lead is sold with the CD or DVD; it should even be included with "bare" drives. This is the other end of the cable we connected between the PCI slots.

Figure 6.51
Connecting the stereo lead to the DVD

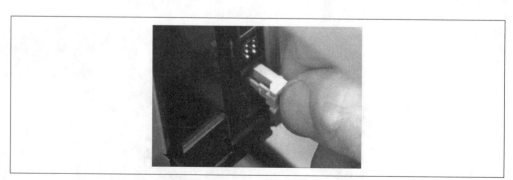

We connect the ribbon cable for the DVD to the secondary IDE controller on the motherboard and to the back of the drive, just like we did with the hard drive. Due to the large number of drive connections coming up in our IDE RAID and SCSI options, we'll skip forward to connecting the power lead to the DVD.

Figure 6.52
Connecting power
to the DVD

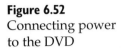

Figure 6.52
Connecting power
to the DVD

At this point our basic Pentium 4 build is finished, and you can skip to step 8.

Option 1: An IDE RAID

We install our Adaptec 1200A RAID controller in the open PCI slot. The adapter is jumperless, but it comes with its own BIOS, just like the motherboard. This software is reached by pressing CTRL+H while the system is starting and provides the basic array configuration. The subject of configuring and managing arrays is beyond the scope of this book; the controller ships with its own 68-page booklet.

Figure 6.53
Installing the
Adaptec RAID
controller

Secure the adapter with a screw. Note that if you connect the hard drive activity LED that normally connects to the motherboard to the adapter, it will only show activity when the RAID drives are being accessed. In addition to the BIOS software, the adapter ships with operating system drivers on CD, which also must be installed.

Figure 6.54
Securing the
RAID controller

We will build a two-drive RAID 1 array that employs mirroring for data security. We begin by attaching the 80-wire ribbon cable to the IDE 1 connector. The blue connector goes to the controller and the black to the drive, just as if it were being attached to the motherboard.

Figure 6.55
Attaching the
ribbon cable to the
IDE 1 connector

As we connect the ribbon cable to the hard drive that was the boot drive in our basic build, you can see that we have installed another identical hard drive in the second cage. Pairs of hard drives in RAIDs must be identical, although you can use different pairs for the master and slave sets if you want.

Figure 6.56
Installing the
ribbon cable to
the boot drive

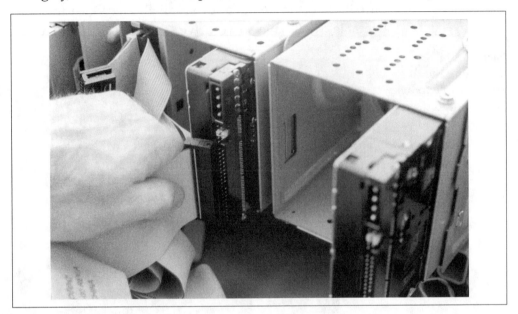

We attach another 80-conductor ribbon cable to the IDE 2 connector. The 1200A shipped with two identical cables, which we would normally use, but we had an identical cable of a different color available, which makes the picture a little clearer. Our RAID 1 array increases performance when the array is read, as different stripes of data can be read from both drives simultaneously, but the performance during writes is unaffected, because all the data must be written to both drives.

Figure 6.57
Attaching the
second ribbon
cable to the RAID
controller

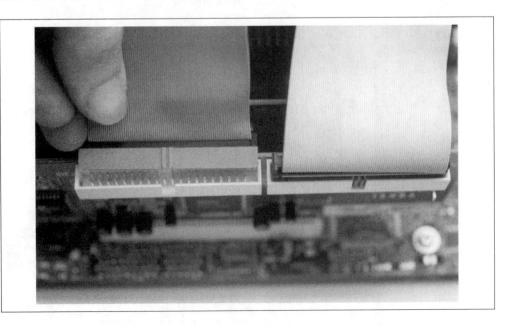

We install the black connector on the end of the IDE 1 ribbon cable to the second hard drive. Both drives must be jumpered as master, which is the default position for the white jumper as shipped from the factory. One of the features of the RAID BIOS software is to allow us to make a direct copy of the original drive on IDE 1 to the identical drive on IDE 2. Once the RAID is configured as bootable, we'll have a two-drive system with 100 percent data redundancy.

Figure 6.58
Attaching the ribbon cable to the second hard drive

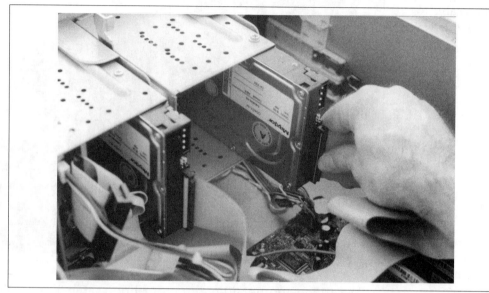

All that remains is to connect the power leads to our two hard drives, and the physical RAID assembly is complete. As soon as the system is booted, you'll need to install the RAID drivers in the operating system for viewing the event log and monitoring. Some of the RAID features are actually transparent to the operating system and can be configured either with the BIOS software or in the operating system.

Figure 6.59
Completed RAID hardware installation

The RAID level is selected at the top of the screen and the drive status is shown at the bottom. The options hidden behind the RAID level selection box are

1. Create Array.

2. Delete Array.

3. Create/Delete Spare.

4. Select Boot Disk.

Figure 6.60
Adaptec
ATA RAID
configuration
screen

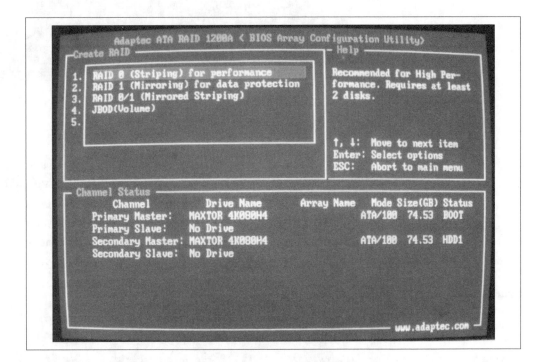

Option 2: A SCSI Subsystem

As discussed in the introductory chapters, a SCSI controller adds a whole new bus to your PC. Adaptec is far and away the dominant player in the SCSI controller market, and this Model 19160 supports Ultra SCSI with speeds up to 160 MB/s. The adapter is equipped with a high-speed 68-pin LVD/SE controller, and an older 50-pin Ultra SE connector. Don't mix high-speed and low-speed devices on the LVD controller, or the card will default to the lower speed.

Figure 6.61
Installing the
Adaptec 19160
SCSI controller

We'll skip showing the securing of the adapter with a screw (believe me, I took the picture) and move on to installing our SCSI drives. We chose to leave our IDE boot drive in place, and install two SCSI drives in the second cage. The thin drive at the top of the cage is a 30 GB Maxtor Atlas 10K, a 10,000 RPM super high performance drive. The thick drive at the bottom is an old-fashioned Fujitsu, which we included to illustrate the slow speed connector.

Figure 6.62
Installing the
drive cage with
two SCSI hard
drives

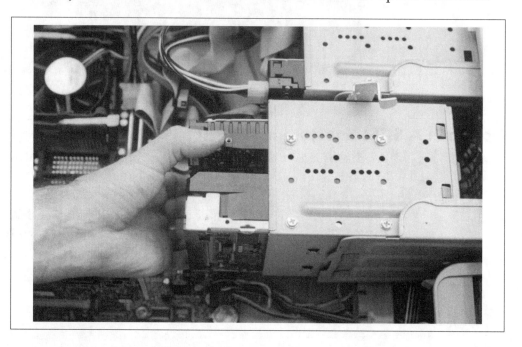

SCSI devices all have a set of SCSI ID jumpers, which is how the controller addresses them and prioritizes requests. The ID jumpers, four on new SCSI devices and three on the older ones, use binary selection. No jumper installed on an ID pair is a 0, a jumper is a 1. For older devices, ignore the leading 0 and use the top row. Also note that by default, SCSI controllers reserve ID 7 for themselves, which is assigned the highest priority. Bootable SCSI drives are traditionally given an ID of 0.

Jumpers	0000	0001	0010	0011	0100	0101	0110	0111
SCSI ID	0	1	2	3	4	5	6	7
Jumpers	1000	1001	1010	1011	1100	1101	1110	1111
SCSI ID	8	9	10	11	12	13	14	15

Figure 6.63
SCSI ID 5 selected on the Atlas 10K hard drive

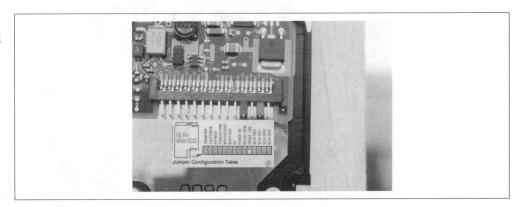

We begin by installing the 68-wire LVD cable to the SCSI adapter. Due to the trapezoidal shape of the connector, it's nearly impossible to get it on backward. However, you still want to take a good look and line it up correctly, because the high density leads to thinner pins, which can get bent if you bash away blindly.

Figure 6.64
Connecting the LVD cable to the Ultra160 connector

The end connector on the SCSI cable is then attached to the Atlas 10K drive, where it can only connect one way. Note the black terminator at the end of the cable that provides termination to the SCSI bus. When you purchase SCSI drives for this type of installation, don't pick a drive with a "hot swap" connector. These require special frame kits so the drive can be inserted or removed through the front of the case, and the drive sports a single connector to the frame kit, which is in turn wired to the standard SCSI and power cables.

Figure 6.65
Attaching the LVD ribbon cable to the Maxtor Atlas 10K drive

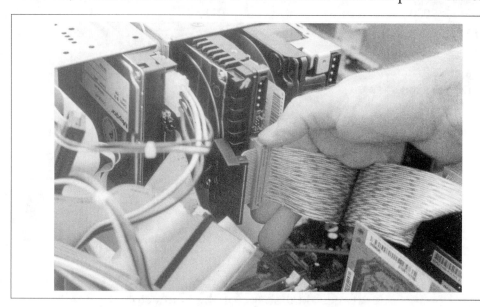

The old style 50-pin SCSI ribbon cable is attached to the SCSI controller. This controller actually provides two new physical buses to the system, each following its own termination rules, but they are combined as a single logical bus when it comes to device IDs. Termination on the controller is enabled by default. The LVD cable comes with a terminator at the end of the cable, but this 50-pin ribbon cable is unterminated.

Figure 6.66
Attaching the 50-pin ribbon cable to the Ultra SE connector

We attach the other end of our ribbon cable to the old Fujitsu drive, whose connector is keyed just like IDE drives. Jumpers on the circuit board of the Fujitsu have been set with a SCSI ID and to enable termination. Some very old SCSI devices actually came equipped with resistor packs that were removed if no termination was required.

Figure 6.67
Connecting the 50-wire ribbon cable to the Fujitsu drive

We skip past the power connectors again to show the completed SCSI installation. The SCSI adapter ships with several instruction booklets and software for a variety of functions, such as managing SCSI tape drives and writing to SCSI CD recorders. If the ribbon cables hadn't been banded up, this case would be an incredible mess. PC manufacturers use special plastic clips for banding ribbon cables, which can often be found at stores like Radio Shack.

Figure 6.68
Completed SCSI installation

The BIOS on the SCSI adapter is accessed by hitting CTRL+A when the system is powered up. All the default values can be changed, but it's not advisable unless you have a conflict or a compatibility issue with older SCSI devices. In the advanced settings, the communications parameters for each logical unit can be set independently.

Figure 6.69
SCSI configuration
screen

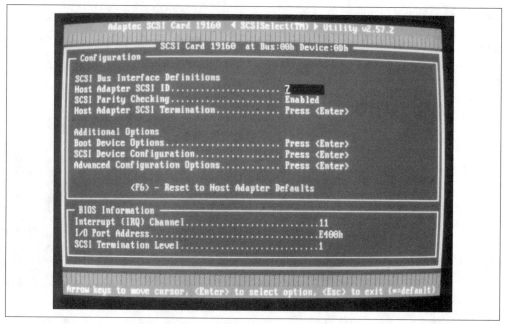

The status of all SCSI devices can also be viewed in the SCSI select utility. The most common error in assembling SCSI systems is setting ID jumpers improperly so that two devices share the same ID. This utility reports an error in that case and normally shows neither device as being present.

Figure 6.70
SCSI device status

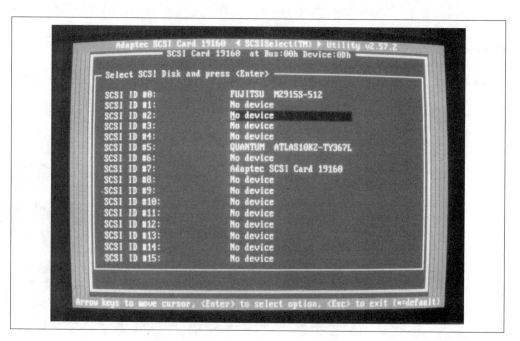

Step 8: Finishing Up

Let's take a final look at the front of our case with the cover open. The three extra drive bays could be used for drives in frame kits, but in business and classrooms, they are often used for multiple CD drives. Such drives can be accessed over the network, and in the classroom environment the front door can be locked so the kids can't fool around with them.

Figure 6.71
Front view of
finished system

The case side or lid is installed the same way it came out and secured with two screws from the back. We decided to lock out the release handle once the lid was installed, just for the sake of illustration. There are a finite variety of these circular keys, so they don't provide any great protection.

Figure 6.72
Locking out the
release handle

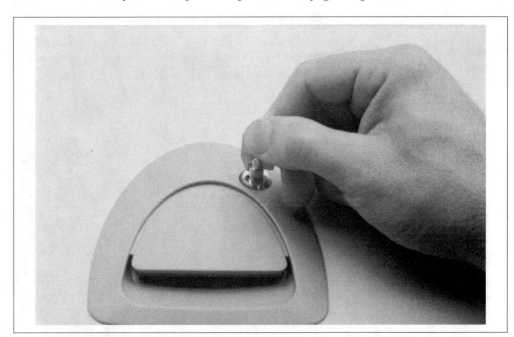

One of the last steps before plugging in the power supply is to check the voltage selector. We chose this system to show the switch in the wrong position for the U.S., 230V, because it was actually sold to us this way! Turning on the PC with the wrong voltage selection will damage the power supply if you're lucky, and much more if you're not.

Figure 6.73
Checking the voltage selector

We're using a large paper clip here to slide the selector switch until the 115V appears. Also note that the rocker switch to the left of the voltage selector is in the "0" down, or off position. Once the system is plugged in, you can set the switch to 1 and leave it permanently on. The logic switch on the front of the PC is used to turn the PC on and off.

Figure 6.74
Setting the voltage to 115V

The main screen of the Intel Setup Utility shows our Pentium 4, with a 400 MHz system bus, 256 KB of CPU cache, and two 128 MB PC800 RIMMs.

Figure 6.75
Intel BIOS
Setup Utility

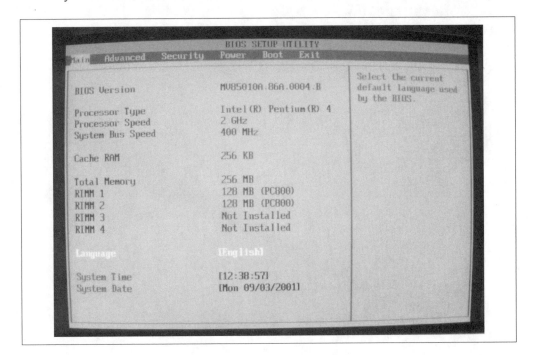

Chapter 7

Installing an Operating System

For the time being, the majority of PC builders will end up installing some version of Microsoft Windows on their PCs. Our example installation is Windows XP, the latest version of Windows available at press time. Windows XP is available in both business and home editions. We will install the home edition here. The 64-bit processors in this book will benefit from the 64-bit version of Windows XP, currently in Beta, that should be commercially available in 2005. Other versions of Windows still in use include Windows Me, Windows 2000, and Windows 98 SE (Second Edition). The primary alternative to Windows is the freeware Linux operating system. Linux is *open source* software, meaning the actual software modules that make up the Linux operating system are available for programmers to modify. The Linux community is constantly posting enhancements and compatibility fixes on the Internet for free download. There are also several branded versions of Linux that come with extras such as phone support and installation CDs.

Since the advent of the bootable CD, all operating system installs have been rendered more or less the same. If the PC you are building is destined to be a server, you may want to have the IP (Internet Protocol) address handy as you install the software to save a step later. However, the only thing you really need to install an operating system is the serial number that ships with the CD. The trick comes after the operating system is installed and you start installing the drivers for specific hardware components, such as the motherboard and the video card. These components are sold with CDs, which often contain drivers for every bit of hardware that manufacturer sells, so just finding the correct driver on the CD can be frustrating. The best way I've found to install drivers from a CD is to skip by Windows requests for drivers by clicking Cancel and run the install software on the driver CD. We offer some solutions for failed operating system installs in the next chapter.

If your boot drive will be a SCSI drive or a RAID, you'll need to supply Windows XP (or any other version of Windows) with the software drivers provided by the motherboard manufacturer or the SCSI or RAID adapter before Windows can install to that drive or RAID. When the message "Press F6 if you need to install third party SCSI or RAID drive" appears, press F6 and insert a floppy disk containing the drivers (you may have to obtain these from the Internet).

The first Windows XP Setup screen offers three options: Setup Windows XP, Repair a Damaged Installation Using Repair Console, or Quit. The difference between a fresh setup and repairing a damaged installation is that if you have already installed XP and invested time in customizing, but have now lost some functionality, repairing should leave your customizations intact.

Figure 7.1
Initial Setup screen

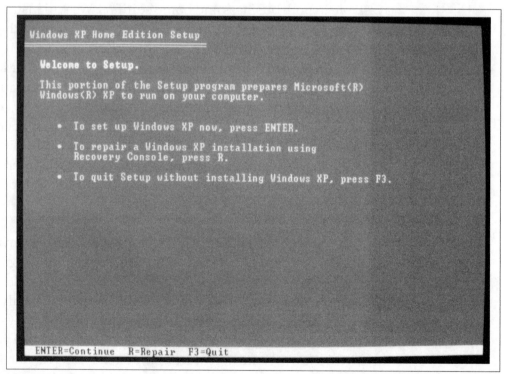

You have two choices when it comes to the Windows Licensing Agreement: you can agree to accept it or not. If you agree, the installation continues; if you don't, the installation is over. It's been a long, long time since I actually read the Licensing Agreement before accepting it.

Figure 7.2
Windows
Licensing
Agreement

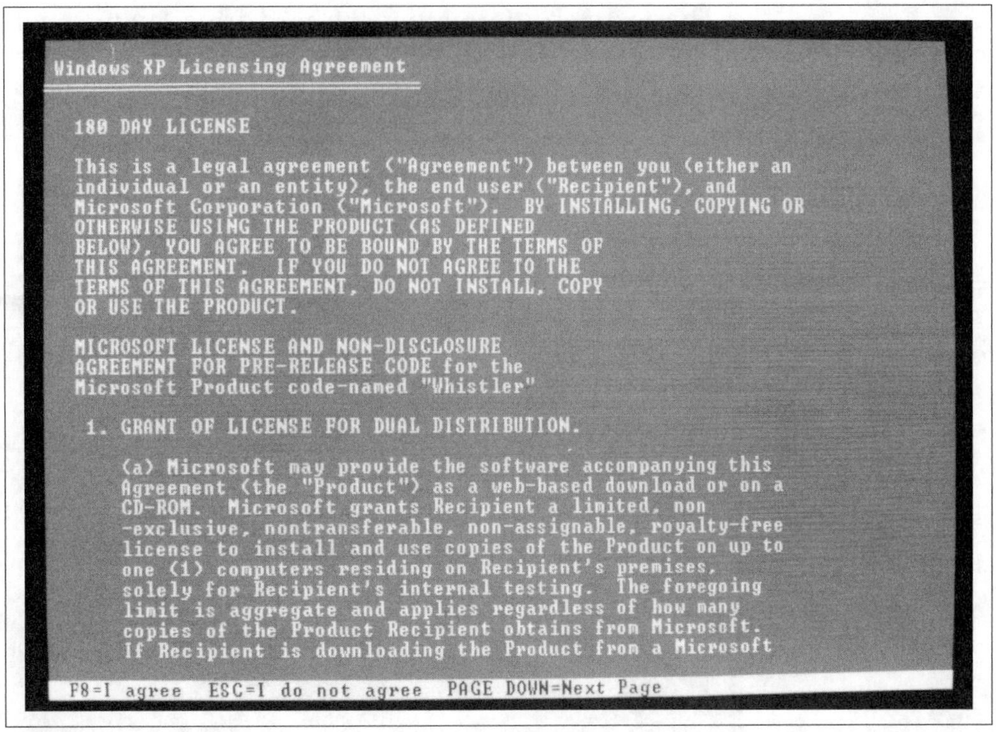

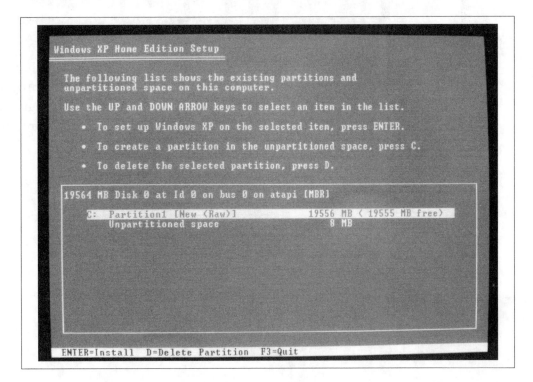

We don't have any reason to create multiple partitions on our hard drive, so we create a single partition using all of the drive space. As soon as you press ENTER, the PC restarts and you are prompted to choose which partition to install XP on. Because you only have one partition, it's an easy choice.

Figure 7.3
Configuring the
hard drive space

The next step is formatting the hard drive, laying down the basic structure for storing and retrieving files. The two choices are NTFS (New Technology File System) and FAT (File Allocation Table), with NTFS being the preferred choice. The quality of new hard drives is such that you can do a Quick Format, which lays down the structure without writing to every location on the drive.

Figure 7.4
Choosing the
format type

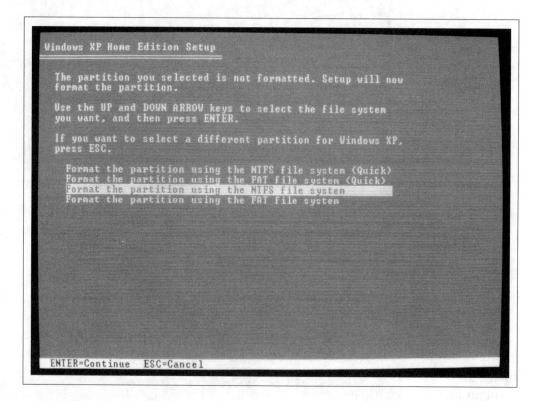

We did a traditional format, which took more than half an hour on a 20 GB hard drive. Microsoft does provide this exciting progress bar for our viewing pleasure. Immediately after the format, XP begins copying installation files to the hard drive, a process that is also accompanied by a progress bar.

Figure 7.5
Formatting
the hard drive

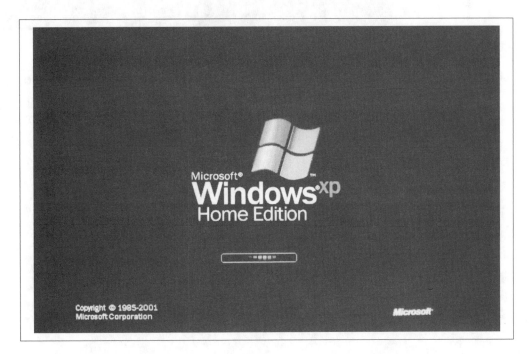

As soon as the copying process is complete, XP restarts the PC again. For some reason, Windows always give you a countdown to an automatic restart with the option to press any key and restart immediately. Once the PC restarts, it boots from the hard drive, rather than from the CD.

Figure 7.6
Windows XP
splash screen

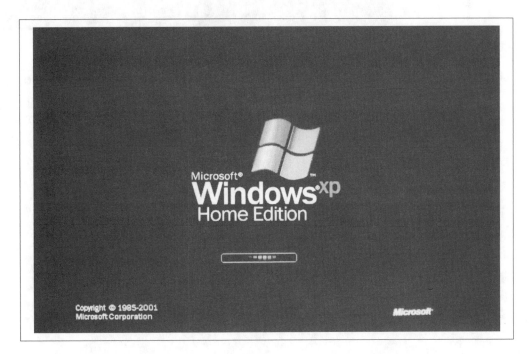

You've passed all the preparatory steps now and have arrived at actually installing the operating system. The first step is to choose regional and language options; later screens will include setting the date and time, networking preferences, keyboard and mouse types, and so forth. This is a common place for the installation to fail if there is a problem with reading the CD drive.

Figure 7.7
Regional settings

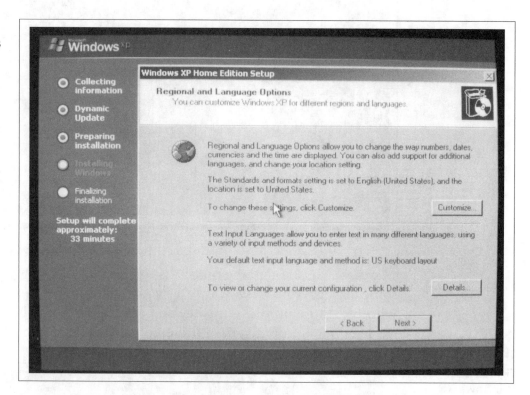

The next screen prompts you for your name (not the computer name) and the organization name. This is strictly registration information. You'll have a chance to configure computer name, and networking workgroup or domain name later.

Figure 7.8
Registration
information

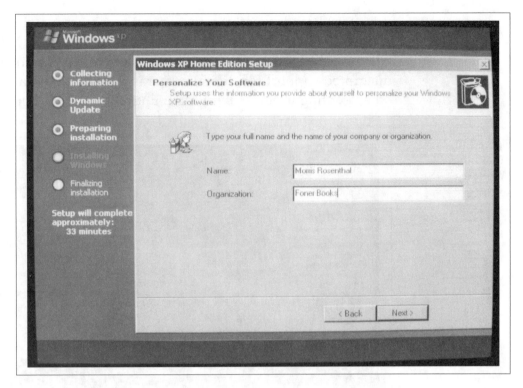

The product key is found on the envelope the install CD shipped in, although earlier and customized versions of Windows might ship with the serial number on the back of the installation booklet or on a separate license agreement. It's extremely easy to make a typing error entering the 25-character long code; in fact, I rarely get it right on the first go.

Figure 7.9
Entering the
serial number

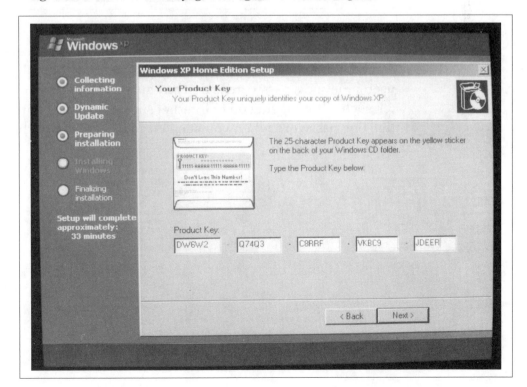

After XP leads you through a couple more screens, similar to Figure 7-7, it saves all these settings. The home edition of Windows XP is positioned as a home entertainment enhancement over earlier Windows versions, with integrated support for digital cameras and multimedia. It also sports another exciting progress bar on the bottom left of the screen.

Figure 7.10
Finalizing
Windows
settings

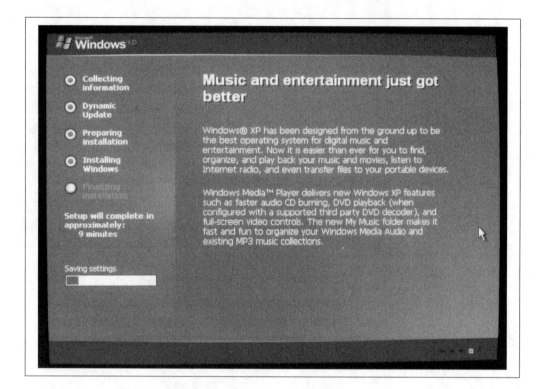

All Windows operating systems support multiple users who can be assigned passwords. The advantage of logging on to Windows with a username and a password is that any subsequent passwords you need to enter, such as for logging on to Internet sites, can be saved in a list. By entering that one password when you start Windows, all your other passwords will be remembered.

Figure 7.11
Adding user names

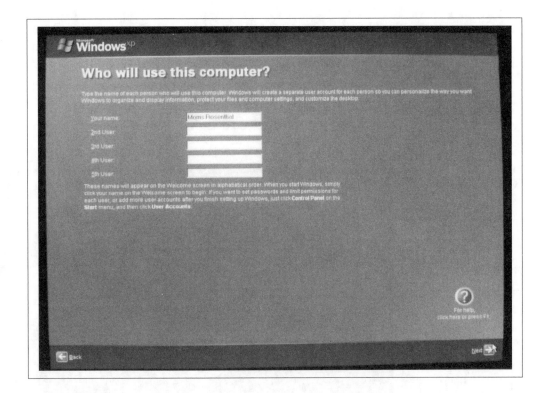

Windows XP has replaced the old blue sky and clouds of previous Windows versions with a pastoral scene, which still includes blue sky and clouds. The Start menu has also been reorganized with what is intended to be a more user-friendly interface, but to the majority of users who are familiar with older Windows versions, it's just window dressing.

Figure 7.12
XP Start menu

The most important feature for the PC builder and troubleshooter in any version of Windows is the Control Panel. The XP Control Panel is poorly organized for this purpose, but you can display the Classic Control Panel, which has looked the same since Windows 95. Within the Classic Control Panel, Device Manager, which is accessed through the System icon, is the place to go for hardware troubleshooting.

Figure 7.13
XP Control Panel

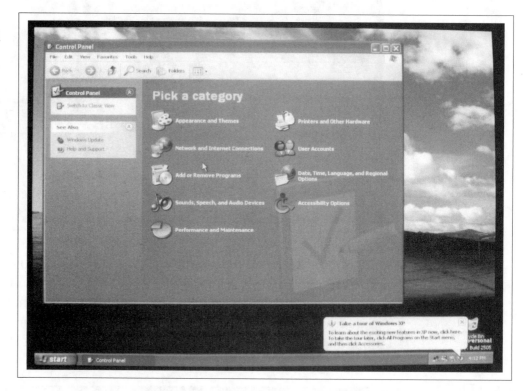

Chapter 8

Troubleshooting Checklists

The first step in troubleshooting your new PC is to double-check that you followed the assembly guidelines in Chapter 3. As stressed in that chapter, the most common problem with any new PC build is partially made or improper connections. Most of the troubleshooting procedures in this chapter require that the cover be removed from the PC and that some components be removed or reconnected. For this reason, it's best to plug in the PC through a switched power strip, so you can use the power strip switch to isolate the system from the electrical supply before every repair attempt.

Most people, even professional technicians, tend to get a little sloppy when troubleshooting, often accidentally introducing a new problem to replace the old. The main key to any type of troubleshooting is to go one step at a time. That way, when the original problem is corrected, you'll know exactly what did the trick, and if you create a new problem, you'll know what went wrong.

We will address five basic scenarios in this chapter, ranging from a stone dead system to a lack of functionality, such as a modem that won't connect. Although these procedures will uncover most assembly errors, there is often no way to isolate a dead component without having other known good parts to swap out. In the world of professional PC troubleshooting and repair, the "Swap 'til you drop" strategy is still the most common troubleshooting technique employed. Swapping components requires no expensive diagnostics software or hardware, and is usually the quickest way to isolate a problem. Another reason to steer clear of specialized diagnostics tools is that they are geared to identifying problems with sub-components that can't be fixed anyway. Finding out exactly which address is bad in the system RAM or in the cache memory of a drive or motherboard is of little use when you'll have to replace the whole assembly anyway.

These troubleshooting procedures are for a newly built PC. If you have been using the PC for some time, for any new problem that arises you have to consider the possibility of a computer virus. One way to check whether you have a hardware problem or a virus problem at boot time is to boot from your original operating system CD. If you do contract a virus, there are many virus doctor programs you can buy with a reasonable certainty they will fix the problem, but you may need Internet access to download the latest virus inoculations from the software manufacturer's web site.

In general, if you encounter a serious recurring software problem with your PC, and you have good backups of any important data, the most reliable fix is to wipe clean the hard drive by deleting the primary partition with the FDISK program and reinstall the software from scratch. Just be really sure you have the original CDs and serial numbers for all the software you use, in addition to good data backups, because once you FDISK, it's all gone. Before running FDISK, confirm that your operating system CD will boot!

CAUTION: We cannot reiterate enough times that you should disconnect power from the system before making any change inside the case, then reconnect after each change to check the result. If you smell a burnt electronics odor at any time, you have a blown component and should not attempt powering up again until it is found and replaced, and the cause of the failure is determined.

Scenario 1: Stone Dead

You switch on your new system and there are no signs of life. The power supply fan doesn't turn, there are no sounds, no lights.

❑ Make sure the power cord is fully inserted into the power supply, that the override switch on the back of the supply (if so equipped) is turned on, that the voltage switch is set correctly. Don't neglect to make sure the wall socket you are plugged into is live by unplugging the computer and plugging in a radio or lamp to check.

❏ Recheck the motherboard documentation for the proper connection of the leads from the front panel power switch. Don't settle for just looking at the switch connection to the motherboard; remove the lead, check that the terminal block matches the documentation, and then reconnect it. Undo the main power supply connection to the motherboard (this requires pressing in the clasp as you pull gently on the connector), inspect the connector for damage, and reconnect. On Pentium 4 systems make sure you have connected the additional 12V header.

❏ Search for shorted components by disconnecting the power and data cables from the drives, one drive at a time, retrying power-up after each drive is disconnected. Without reconnecting the drives, remove each adapter card (leave video for last) one at a time, retrying power-up after each removal.

❏ Remove and reinstall memory DIMMs or RIMMs, inspecting for physical damage. Remove and reinstall the heatsink and CPU, double-checking the CPU fan is connected to the proper terminal on the motherboard. Never attempt to power up the system without the heatsink installed.

❏ In extremely rare cases, the power switch on the front panel may be faulty. You can use a continuity checker or Ohm-meter to check the switch or you can carefully—*carefully*—take a screwdriver with an insulated handle and momentarily short the two pins where the switch lead connects to the motherboard. Although the switch works on low voltage, you might be startled if the machine comes on and rake the screwdriver tip across the motherboard, so don't try this unless you have some experience working with live systems.

❏ Remove the motherboard from the case and check for loose screws, extra standoffs, and anything else that could cause a short circuit to the motherboard circuitry. Reinstall the motherboard in the case and reinstall the video adapter, then try powering up.

If you still have no power, the problem is most likely a defective power supply or defective motherboard.

Scenario 2: Power Comes On; Screen Is Dead

You hear the power come on and the drives spinning up, but the screen remains blank.

❏ Make sure the monitor is plugged into a good power outlet by switching wall sockets with the power supply cord. If the power cord is not permanently attached to the monitor, make sure it is fully inserted in the socket on the back of the monitor. If your monitor is equipped with manual dials for brightness and contrast, make sure they are in the middle of their range.

❏ Remove the monitor connector from the video card and check that none of the pins in the shell are bent over. Note that some missing pins in the three-row high-density connector are normal.

❏ Remove and reseat the video adapter, making sure the hold-down screw doesn't cause the back end of the adapter to lift partially out of the slot.

❏ Check for a defective or conflicting adapter on the bus. Remove any other adapters installed, one by one, rechecking power-up after each. Don't forget to unplug the power supply, or turn off the power strip or override switch before each removal.

❏ Double-check the motherboard documentation for overlooked CPU selection switches or jumpers settings. Depending on the motherboard used, CPU selection might be automatic. Don't take the manual at its word that the default settings are set; check the actual switch and jumper positions on the motherboard.

❏ Double-check that CPU and memory modules are seated properly, particularly slot-type CPUs, which can take a good deal of pressure to mate correctly with the motherboard.

If you still have no live screen, the problem is likely defective hardware. Make sure the case speaker is properly connected to the motherboard as per the motherboard documentation. If you hear a series of beeps, note the number and sequence, as they will pinpoint the defective component. The motherboard documentation or manufacturer web site should give the codes, although the most likely candidates for beeps on a dead screen are the video adapter or the RAM. If no beeps sound, the most likely candidates are a dead monitor (easily checked by connecting it to another system), a defective motherboard, or a defective power supply. In some instances, you may have bad RAM or a bad video adapter, but still not hear any beep codes.

Scenario 3: Screen Comes On; No Boot

You get text appearing on the screen, but the PC either won't try to boot or locks up in the process.

❏ No onscreen messages indicating boot failure.

    ❏ Enter CMOS Setup by following onscreen instructions (usually by pressing the DEL or F1 key) after power-up. Select the CMOS option to Restore Default Settings or similarly phrased option, save, and reboot. *Note:* If you cannot access Setup, double-check that the keyboard and mouse connectors aren't interchanged. If you still can't access setup, disconnect power and remove all adapters except the video and disconnect the drives. If you still can't access Setup you have some defective hardware, most likely the motherboard or keyboard, though it could still be the RAM or CPU. The core components should always be bought from the same source to simplify return issues.

    ❏ If there are still no messages indicating boot failure, enter CMOS Setup again and make sure the CPU speed setting, the bus clock frequency, and the IDE interface speed don't exceed your components ratings.

    ❏ If the system hangs at Verifying DMI Data Pool, it is usually a motherboard or an older IDE device problem. If you have an option to enable Reset Configuration Data, use it. Disconnect your IDE cables from the motherboard and see if you can get as far as a Drive Failure or No Boot Device message. If not, the motherboard will probably need replacing, although you can try discharging the onboard battery first by using the jumper setting in the motherboard manual for disabling a forgotten password.

❏ Missing operating system or no boot device message.

    ❏ Check that the IDE or serial ATA cables are connected to the drives and motherboard properly by removing and reinstalling them. Make sure the power connectors to all of the drives are properly installed. Make sure the master/slave jumpers for older IDE drives are installed properly or set to CS (Cable Select) on an 80-wire ribbon cable.

    ❏ If the system tries to boot a CD and fails, it may just be bad timing. Strangely enough, some high-speed CD drives take so long to get up to speed that the BIOS (motherboard logic) gives up on them before they get there. If the screen displays a message such as "Insert CD and hit any key when ready," eject the CD tray; then push it back in, but wait until you hear the drive spin up before striking a key to continue. It might take a few efforts to get this right if it's going to work.

❑ Check that the operating system CD is readable in another system, and don't try using pirated operating system software on home-recorded CDs.

❑ Enter CMOS Setup and rearrange the boot sequence so that the CD-ROM or the IDE channel to which it is connected is selected as the first boot device. This shouldn't be necessary, but it will help if a previous attempt to install the operating system failed, leaving the hard drive appearing bootable to the motherboard.

❑ If you are using older IDE drives, simplify the system by removing any additional drives so all you have left are a "master" hard drive on the primary IDE channel and a "master" CD on the secondary IDE channel. If it doesn't work, as a final check try both drives on the primary controller with the CD as the "slave."

Scenario 4: Boots; Locks Up During or After OS Install

Everything appears to be working fine, right up through formatting the hard drive. But, at some point during the operating system installation or immediately after, the PC locks up.

❑ First check with your parts vendor or operating system manufacturer for known compatibility issues. Also be aware that some CDRs and combination drives have problems with operating system install, which usually manifests itself as a "read error."

❑ All modern motherboards should have a "Hardware Monitoring" screen or the equivalent available through CMOS Setup (see Figure 5-71 in Chapter 5). Check that the power supply voltages are stable (flip-flopping between two set values is normal) and that the CPU temperature is within its operating range.

❑ Unplug the power and remove all adapters except the video adapter. Install the operating system. Next install the motherboard drivers from the CD that shipped with the motherboard and the video adapter driver from its own CD. Install any other adapters one at a time, reconnect power and reboot, allowing the operating system to deal with them individually.

❏ Make sure you are using the approved cabling for any high-performance parts such as 80-conductor ribbon cables with ATA 100 or ATA 133 IDE hard drives, because communication breakdowns at high speeds are likely to show up under the load of operating system installation.

❏ In some rare cases, operating system installation can fail repeatedly because a borderline component is suffering a heat-related failure as the system warms up. This is extremely difficult to troubleshoot without parts to swap out, and if you bring the parts back to the point of purchase, it might be hard to convince the vendor that the problem isn't in your imagination. Make sure the CPU heatsink is properly installed, that the heatsink fan is working, and that you aren't building the system in a hot attic in the summer. Go through the steps related to CMOS Setup in Scenario 3 and document all the troubleshooting steps you go through for the vendor. Try reinstalling the operating system several times with no adapter other than video before concluding that you have a hardware failure.

Scenario 5: Boots and Runs

If your operating system installation goes smoothly but you have trouble accessing a particular device, the problem is as likely to be software as hardware. Extensive software troubleshooting is outside the scope of this book, but we will mention some of the key points you can check in Windows operating systems.

Floppy Drive

❏ If the activity light on the front of the floppy drive stays lit all the time, the ribbon cable on the drive or the motherboard is probably backward.

❏ If the drive is not detected properly by CMOS Setup or recognized by the operating system, either the ribbon cable or power cord is partially or improperly connected (see Chapter 3), or the drive or a cable is bad. Replace the ribbon cable and try another power supply lead if one is available.

❏ For any problems reading or writing specific floppy disks, either the disk is bad, or the drive that wrote the disk is incompatible with the drive trying to read it due to head alignment issues. Both of these problems are super-common and I've seen a 30 percent failure rate on brand-new "100 percent certified" floppy disks.

Hard Drive

❏ Any message indicating a hard drive read or write failure is a hardware error. Try replacing the data cable, making sure you use the newer 80-conductor type for IDE drives or a quality serial ATA cable for serial ATA drives.

❏ For non-SATA drives, try isolating the boot hard drive on its own IDE channel, moving any other drives to the secondary channel on their own cable or temporarily disconnecting them. For SATA drives, try using a different motherboard connector (channel) for the boot drive, and make sure it's selected for boot in CMOS.

❏ If the hard drive is excessively noisy or makes a continual clunking sound, it has suffered internal damage and odds are even an expensive data recovery outfit won't be able to help.

❏ If the errors persist, either the drive or controller is bad. If you can disable the motherboard drive controller (all channels), you can try substituting a PCI drive controller before giving up on the motherboard. You can also try lowering the transfer speed in CMOS Setup, but if the problem goes away, you are sacrificing performance.

CD or DVD Drive

❏ If the drive has trouble reading a particular disc, try wiping off any fingerprints with a clean flannel shirt. Note rewriteable discs written in CDRs and DVDRs are often unreadable in other drives.

❏ For continual read errors, try all of the steps for hard drive troubleshooting: new IDE cable, isolation, and swapping IDE controller. CD and DVD drives are far less standardized than hard drives, so isolating them on their own controller will often fix the problem.

❏ If you can't play music CDs even though your speakers work with other computer sounds, the thin audio cable from the sound card (or motherboard with integrated sound) to the four-pin connector on the back of the drive is improperly installed or missing.

❏ If you record music CDs on your PC and they won't play in your stereo, make sure you are using CDR blanks, not CDRW.

❏ If you have a CDR or DVDR and your write sessions often fail, try recording at a lower speed and make sure you are using media certified for at least the speed at which you are recording.

Modem

❑ Check that the phone line from the wall goes into the modem jack labeled "line." Plug a regular handset into the modem jack labeled phone. If you don't hear a dial tone, either the modem or the phone line is dead.

❑ In Windows, go to Start | Settings | Control Panel | Modems | Diagnostics | More Info. If your modem doesn't show up in Windows, power down and try removing all of the other adapters except the video card from the PC before rebooting. If Windows still doesn't find your modem, try it in a different motherboard slot. If Windows still can't find the modem, it is probably defective or incompatible.

❑ If you hear the modem dial but the only thing that happens is that after a while the operator picks up, you are probably dialing tone on a pulse system.

❑ If you never get connect speeds over 33K, contact your Internet service provider with your modem information.

❑ If you connect between 33K and 53K but with inconsistent speed and frequent disconnects, you probably have an aging or overloaded local phone infrastructure. Try another phone jack in your house in case it is a just a poorly wired outlet. Try using the modem outside of business hours, particularly morning and after school, when traffic is heaviest.

❑ Don't daisy-chain too many phone devices, such as fax to computer to computer. The weakest link in the telephone infrastructure is the RJ-11 jack on the ends of the short phone cords you connect from device to device.

Sound Card

❑ Check Windows Device Manager to see whether there are any conflicts and be sure the sound card drivers are installed. Device Manager can be invoked either through Control Panel | System or by *right-clicking* (right-hand mouse button) My Computer and choosing Properties. If Windows didn't recognize the sound card, try powering down and removing the other adapters, except the video card from the PC before rebooting. If Windows still doesn't find your sound card, try it in a different motherboard slot. If it still can't find the sound card, it probably is defective or incompatible.

❑ Make sure your speakers are plugged into the correct jack on the sound card, because the little pictures can be deceptively similar. The speaker jack usually is the one right above the game port. Make sure speakers with an external power source are plugged in and turned on, and that the volume dial isn't off.

❑ If you have been using your PC for a while and then lose all sound, the most common reason is the "mute" box being mysteriously checked in one of the innumerable mixer panels that install with sound card software. Happy hunting!

Network

❑ If the network adapter doesn't appear in Device Manager, try powering down and removing the other adapters, except the video card, from the PC before rebooting. If Windows still doesn't find your network adapter, try it in a different motherboard slot. If it still can't find the adapter, it probably is defective or incompatible.

❑ If the card looks healthy in Device Manager but you can't connect to your local network, check all the software protocols and identification settings in Start | Settings | Control Panel | Network. For home networks, getting the Workgroup name wrong is the most common error.

❑ If you are sure you have all your software settings right by comparing them line for line with another PC on the network, you have a cabling problem. Most small networks are wired for 10/100 BaseT, but the cables are often built incorrectly. 10BaseT and 100BaseTX use four conductors in two pairs in an RJ-45 connector, 1&2 and 3&6. Some other standards use all eight wires in four pairs, but the important point in every case is that 3 and 6 must utilize a color-coded pair, something many cable makers still neglect.

Video

❑ If the screen seems jumpy, particularly from a distance, it could be the monitor itself. Another possibility is interference from electrical equipment, such as an external transformer for speakers or other device resting near the speaker. In industrial environments, electrical wiring in walls carrying high currents can cause wavy interference.

❑ If you look at the screen out of the corner of your eye and it seems to flash near the edges or bottom, the vertical refresh frequency is probably too low. You can try a lower screen resolution or changing video modes if the video card software gives you that option.

❑ If you are missing a primary color, check the 15-pin video connector to see whether any of the pins are bent over. If not, you have probably lost one of the electron guns in the monitor, requiring warranty repair. Loss of vertical hold is also a common symptom of a bent or broken connector pin or damaged video cable.

Printers, Scanners, and other External Peripherals

❑ If your printer or other external device can't be detected, make sure you are using a new, approved cable for connecting the device, and that it is plugged in and powered on. Older parallel cables often fail with new printers, even though the connectors match. Many new printers have no power switch, as they are always on and waiting for jobs in a low power mode when plugged in.

❑ Check in CMOS Setup that you have selected the proper port protocol to work with the device. Some printers, scanners, and external drives require you to set the port to ECP (Extended Capability Port) or EPP (Enhanced Parallel Port) for two-way communications and increased speed. The default setting for the printer port in Setup is usually Normal, which doesn't support any of these advanced functions.

❑ If the device is detected but times out, make sure you have followed the unpacking and initial setup instructions, such as unlocking a scanner or properly installing the toner and paper in a printer.

❑ Try using a single power strip to power your PC and all the peripherals to obtain a common ground. You might have a ground loop where current is actually present on the grounds of the signal cables, due to the devices being plugged into different outlets in a room. Sometimes an outlet has a compromised ground, which leaves the PC and the peripheral grounds at different potentials. This can create a current flow that results in unpredictable operation.

Index

INTERNATIONAL CONTACT INFORMATION

AUSTRALIA
McGraw-Hill Book Company
Australia Pty. Ltd.
TEL +61-2-9900-1800
FAX +61-2-9878-8881
http://www.mcgraw-hill.com.au
books-it_sydney@mcgraw-hill.com

CANADA
McGraw-Hill Ryerson Ltd.
TEL +905-430-5000
FAX +905-430-5020
http://www.mcgraw-hill.ca

**GREECE, MIDDLE EAST, & AFRICA
(Excluding South Africa)**
McGraw-Hill Hellas
TEL +30-210-6560-990
TEL +30-210-6560-993
TEL +30-210-6560-994
FAX +30-210-6545-525

MEXICO (Also serving Latin America)
McGraw-Hill Interamericana Editores
S.A. de C.V.
TEL +525-1500-5108
FAX +525-117-1589
http://www.mcgraw-hill.com.mx
carlos_ruiz@mcgraw-hill.com

SINGAPORE (Serving Asia)
McGraw-Hill Book Company
TEL +65-6863-1580
FAX +65-6862-3354
http://www.mcgraw-hill.com.sg
mghasia@mcgraw-hill.com

SOUTH AFRICA
McGraw-Hill South Africa
TEL +27-11-622-7512
FAX +27-11-622-9045
robyn_swanepoel@mcgraw-hill.com

SPAIN
McGraw-Hill/
Interamericana de España, S.A.U.
TEL +34-91-180-3000
FAX +34-91-372-8513
http://www.mcgraw-hill.es
professional@mcgraw-hill.es

**UNITED KINGDOM, NORTHERN,
EASTERN, & CENTRAL EUROPE**
McGraw-Hill Education Europe
TEL +44-1-628-502500
FAX +44-1-628-770224
http://www.mcgraw-hill.co.uk
emea_queries@mcgraw-hill.com

ALL OTHER INQUIRIES Contact:
McGraw-Hill/Osborne
TEL +1-510-420-7700
FAX +1-510-420-7703
http://www.osborne.com
omg_international@mcgraw-hill.com

Sound Off!

Visit us at **www.osborne.com/bookregistration** and let us know what you thought of this book. While you're online you'll have the opportunity to register for newsletters and special offers from McGraw-Hill/Osborne.

We want to hear from you!

Sneak Peek

Visit us today at **www.betabooks.com** and see what's coming from McGraw-Hill/Osborne tomorrow!

Based on the successful software paradigm, Bet@Books™ allows computing professionals to view partial and sometimes complete text versions of selected titles online. Bet@Books™ viewing is free, invites comments and feedback, and allows you to "test drive" books in progress on the subjects that interest you the most.

eBay Your Way to Success

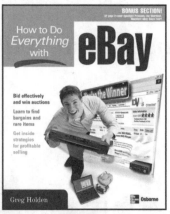
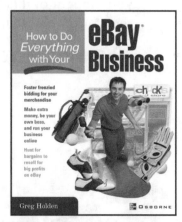